MW00514372

The Man Behind the Beard

It's never too late to realize your Dreams!
~ Candice Smith

The Man Behind the Beard

Pat Ficcio

&

Candice Smith

Softpress Publishing, LLC

SOFTPRESS PUBLISHING
4118 Hickory Crossroads Road
Kenly, NC 27542

Designed by William C. Parker

ISBN-10: 1-7322744-3-6
ISBN-13: 978-1-7322744-3-3

DEDICATION

This book is dedicated to every child, friend, and family member in my life. If you believe, you will receive the pleasures I have shared making you happy.

~ Pat Ficcio

I dedicate this book to all who believe in the Magic of Santa. Those who are Santa's helpers, those who keep Christmas secrets, and those who still look out the window with expectant eyes on Christmas Eve, you are absolutely correct, Santa Claus exists!

~ Candice Smith

SPECIAL ACKNOWLEDGEMENTS

I would like to thank my friends who range in ages from one to 78. It's beautiful to make dreams come true.

Look up at the sky on Christmas Eve and you'll feel, I'm here.

My parents, my father taking me to the Bamberger's Thanksgiving Day Parade.

My late wife, Claire, for my life as Santa.

My son, Tom.

My employer allowing me the time given to me to bring the Spirit of Christmas.

And to God for giving me the health to spread the Joy of the Season.

To my wife, Camille, for making my journey complete by joining me as Mrs. Claus.

~ Pat Ficcio

I would like to thank my parents for helping Santa from the time they had children. They provided the most loving, fulfilling, and wonderful Christmas memories a little girl could ever have.

I would like to thank my in-laws for accepting me into their family with unconditional love and sharing their Christmas Magic and Santa traditions with me.

I would like to thank my three children – Matthew, Gregory, and Rosemilee – for making Christmas magical again for me. They enrich my very soul.

I would like to thank Camille and Pat who entrusted me with their stories, pictures, and legacy. I am honored, humbled, and thrilled to have taken this journey with you. You have me convinced that you really are Santa and Mrs. Claus.

I would like to thank my publisher William Parker who never backs down from a challenge and sees my projects through with love, humor, patience, and professionalism.

~ Candice Smith

CONTENTS

PREFACE

Meeting Santa Claus is perhaps one of the greatest moments in one's life. Waiting in a line, anticipation building, thoughts scattered, or in some hyper-focused thoughts, it's most children's rite of passage. Photo albums and scrap books are filled with formal pictures of children with Santa Claus. From clueless babies to scared toddlers, wide-eyed school-aged children to doubting pre-teens, visiting Santa is as traditional as putting up the family Christmas tree.

But what is it like for Santa Claus? How does he feel looking at the line of children waiting to see him? How does he deal with Herculean requests and doubting Thomases?

For the first time the information is available exclusively.

Santa Claus – also known as Pat Ficcio – and Mrs. Claus – his wife Camille – have been talking to children for decades, hearing wishes, receiving adoring hugs, and being asked endless questions about the North Pole, the toy-making elves, and Santa's diet of cookies and milk.

What keeps Santa in the business of making children happy? For nearly two thousand years Santa has been a part of the fabric of the lives of children. It's in their DNA to believe.

And, once Pat put on the costume, it became apparent to him that being Santa Claus was a calling he would never ignore.

Who was St. Nicholas?

THE MAN BEHIND THE BEARD

How did Saint Nicholas become Santa Claus?

And, how did Pat Ficcio come to be Santa Claus for the last seven decades?

SANTA CLAUS' INTRODUCTION

What was known about the appearance of Santa Claus has morphed throughout the ages.

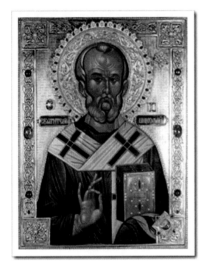

St. Nicholas

The couple who would become Nicholas' parents were wealthy and pious people who yearned for a baby of their own. For years they were childless but kept faith, performed good deeds for the poor, and continued to pray to their Christian god for a child. At last, long into their union, the couple was blessed with a son whom they named Nicholas. Born in 280 A.D. in Asia-Minor (present day Turkey), Nicholas' parents immediately dedicated their miracle baby's life to God. The loving parents entrusted their son's life and spiritual upbringing to the boy's uncle, also Nicholas, a Bishop where the family lived.

Nicholas' parents, being much older when he was born, died of illness before Nicholas reached adulthood. He inherited their wealth but lived a plain life. By the time Nicholas was an adult, he became a

I

priest in the Christian church. He used the monies left to him by his parents to continue to help the poor where he lived.

Based on the location of Nicholas' birth and life, it is logical to conclude that he looked like many who occupy these lands. Many scholars believe Nicholas would have had a complexion typical of the Mediterranean peoples, olive-colored skin and brown eyes. Because of Nicholas' vocation of being a priest, the belief is he was thin, serious, and probably had a beard.

St. Nicholas of Myra

Having been raised in the Church, Nicholas lived a life of service, always helping others in his community. He was a kindly person who had a reputation of being wise.

The most famous story about St. Nicholas, and the genesis of why children traditionally hang up their Christmas stockings for him to fill, goes like this:

> There was a poor man who had three daughters. The man was so poor that he did not have enough money for a dowry, so his daughters couldn't get married. One night, Nicholas secretly dropped a bag of gold down the chimney and into the house allowing for the eldest daughter to marry. The bag fell into a stocking that had been hung by the fire to dry. This was repeated later with the second daughter. Finally, determined to discover the

person who had given him the money, the father secretly hid by the fire every evening until he caught Nicholas dropping in a bag of gold. Nicholas begged the man to not tell anyone what he had done, because he did not want to bring attention to himself. But soon the news got out and when anyone received a secret gift, it was thought that maybe it was from Nicholas.[1]

Nicholas' agreed date of death was December 6 in the year 343 A.D. Nicholas' popularity grew exponentially as people told and retold stories of his kindness and generosity. With each telling, perhaps, more details and embellishments may have been added. It's impossible to know, but Nicholas' reputation and the people's adoration grew so great that he became sainted due to the miracles he was reported to have performed. In fact, he was the most popular saint not mentioned in the Bible. He has numerous churches named after him in Europe, and his image was recreated in artworks more times than any other saint except Mary.

St. Nicholas

As his reputation was so good, Nicholas became the patron saint of many different groups who wanted him to protect them. Among the many, Nicholas was the patron saint of sailing. Centuries after

---

[1] The Man Behind the Story of Father Christmas/Santa Claus. (n.d.). Retrieved from https://www.whychristmas.com/customs/fatherchristmas.shtml#man

his death, the Dutch, a seafaring people, brought their reverence for and adulation of St. Nicholas across the Atlantic when they settled the colony of New Amsterdam.

In addition to the patron saint of sailors, Nicholas' reputation was always attached to children and was associated as a gift bringer as the gold coins story illustrates. His popularity, the people's reliance, and their faith led to celebrations of St. Nicholas on his Feast Day, December 6th.

For nearly three centuries, 1200 to 1500, St. Nicholas was the bringer of gifts with celebrations centered around his day, December 6. Nicholas had taken on characteristics of pagan gods, like the Roman Saturn or the Norse Odin, who were magical figures who, among other talents, could fly, and had similar physical traits of long, white beards. Nicholas became the lightning rod for parents to have a foil to ensure that children lived well-behaved lives by being kind and compassionate, and even saying their prayers.[2]

How St. Nicholas Became Santa Claus

St. Nicholas' popularity seemed unending in Christendom. That all changed once Martin Luther posted his 95 *Theses* on October 31, 1517 in northern Europe. This is the start of what came to be known as The Reformation. Reforms to the Church, different Christian religions forming, and the focus squarely on Jesus Christ for many reformers led to the popularity of St. Nicholas waning.

---

[2] Handwerk, Brian. "From St. Nicholas to Santa Claus: The Surprising Origins of Kris Kringle". (2018, December 25). Retrieved from https://www.nationalgeographic.com/news/2018/12/131219-santa-claus-origin-history-christmas-facts-st-nicholas/

But the tradition of gift giving was so ingrained that someone had to continue to deliver presents to children at Christmas. In the United Kingdom, particularly in England, the gift bringer became "Father Christmas" or "Old Man Christmas." In France, he was known as "Père Nöel."

In some European countries, the gift bringer did not arrive on St. Nicholas' Feast Day of December 6th. This date, according to reformers, had no connection to the Christ child and pulled attention away from Jesus Christ's importance. To realign gift giving with Christmas, the one who brought presents would come on Jesus' birthday. Like St. Nicholas, this was a benevolent gift giver called the "Christkind," a figure who appeared to be a golden-haired baby with wings who represented the baby Jesus.[3]

Christkind would eventually morph into "Kris Kringle" in the United States with those who brought that tradition over from Europe. The Dutch settlers in America took their patron Saint of Children and Sailors, St. Nicholas, and he became "Sinterklaas" which evolved into "Santa Claus."

The first anglicizing of the name to Santa Claus was in a story that appeared in a New York City newspaper in 1773.

St. Nicholas' Day on December 6th is still happily celebrated in places like the Netherlands. Referred to by many as Dutch Christmas, children leave clogs or shoes out on the night of December 5th (St. Nicholas Eve) to be filled with presents. They also

---

[3] The Man Behind the Story of Father Christmas/Santa Claus. (n.d.). Retrieved from https://www.whychristmas.com/customs/fatherchristmas.shtml#man

believe that by leaving some hay and carrots in their shoes for Sinterklaas's horse, they will be left some tasty sweet treats.[4]

St. Nicholas in America

In early America Christmas wasn't celebrated in the same way it is in modern times. The holiday was abandoned in New England as it was against the strict puritanical beliefs of the residents. It was too akin to the pagan celebration of Saturnalia that once occupied its place on the Roman calendar. Raucous drinking, partying, and celebrating marked the holiday. The gift bringer was long forgotten.[5]

Thomas Nast's illustration "A Christmas Furlough" for the front page of an 1863 issue of *Harper's Weekly*

That all changed in the early 1800s when Americans, struggling to find a history to connect that was not English in origin, rediscovered

---

[4] The Man Behind the Story of Father Christmas/Santa Claus. (n.d.). Retrieved from https://www.whychristmas.com/customs/fatherchristmas.shtml#man

[5] Handwerk, Brian. "From St. Nicholas to Santa Claus: The Surprising Origins of Kris Kringle". (2018, December 25). Retrieved from https://www.nationalgeographic.com/news/2018/12/131219-santa-claus-origin-history-christmas-facts-st-nicholas/

the Germanic/Dutch roots of Saint Nicholas/Sinterklaas and began to rewrite the way American families celebrated Christmas.[6]

It seems likely that Saint Nicholas became an American tradition during a wave of interest in Dutch customs following the Revolutionary War.

Washington Irving's 1809 book *Knickerbocker's History of New York* was the first to write about a pipe-smoking Nicholas who took to the skies in a flying wagon, delivering presents to good girls and boys and switches to bad ones.[7] It struck a chord with his readership. It fueled the imagination and passion for Christmas in America. Irving took minor customs and made them part of the fabric of American families for generations. He's responsible for taking Christmas away from a boozy, crazy, debaucherous time and into the home surrounded by family.

John Pintard, founder of the New York Historical Society, delved deeply in the legend, and the Society hosted its first St. Nicholas anniversary dinner in 1810. Artist Alexander Anderson was hired to draw an image of the Saint for the dinner. Nicholas was still shown as a religious figure, but now he was also leaving gifts in children's stockings which were hung by the fireplace to dry, eluding to St.

---

[6] Handwerk, Brian. "From St. Nicholas to Santa Claus: The Surprising Origins of Kris Kringle". (2018, December 25). Retrieved from https://www.nationalgeographic.com/news/2018/12/131219-santa-claus-origin-history-christmas-facts-st-nicholas/

[7] Handwerk, Brian. "From St. Nicholas to Santa Claus: The Surprising Origins of Kris Kringle". (2018, December 25). Retrieved from https://www.nationalgeographic.com/news/2018/12/131219-santa-claus-origin-history-christmas-facts-st-nicholas/

Nicholas' famous acts of charity saving the three daughters with his gifts of gold.[8]

In 1821, an anonymous illustrated poem entitled "The Children's Friend: A New-Year's Present to the Little Ones from Five to Twelve" gave a clear connection to the secular Santa Claus and identifying him with Christmas. This was finally the description of what became Santa Claus. "The Children's Friend," as it became known, re-introduced the magical gift-bringing St. Nicholas, now a non-religious, magical figure, who was dressed in the furs of a Germanic gift bringer.[9]

What makes "The Children's Friend" crucial to the history of Santa Claus in America is the inclusion of illustrations allowing readers to catch a glimpse of the gift bringer. Included among the drawings are Santa's sleigh and reindeer. It also provides evidence that even in the early nineteenth century, New Years was a popular date for Santa's arrival.[10]

---

[8] History.com editors. "Santa Claus". (2018, December 6). Retrieved from https://www.history.com/topics/christmas/santa-claus

[9] Handwerk, Brian. "From St. Nicholas to Santa Claus: The Surprising Origins of Kris Kringle". (2018, December 25). Retrieved from https://www.nationalgeographic.com/news/2018/12/131219-santa-claus-origin-history-christmas-facts-st-nicholas/

[10] "1821: The Children's Friend". (n.d.) Retrieved from http://www.santaswhiskers.com/the-children-s-friend.html

"The Children's Friend"

"Old Santeclaus with much delight
His reindeer drives this frosty night.
O'er chimney tops, and tracks of snow,
To bring his yearly gifts to you.

The steady friend of virtuous youth,
The friend of duty, and of truth,
Each Christmas eve he joys to come
Where love and peace have made their home"

Through many houses he has been,
And various beds and stockings seen,
Some, white as snow, and neatly mended,
Others, that seem'd for pigs intended.

Where e'er I found good girls or boys,
That hated quarrels, strife and noise,
Left an apple, or a tart,
Or wooden gun, or painted cart;

To some I gave a pretty doll,
To some a peg-top, or a ball;
No crackers, cannons, squibs, or rockets,
To blow their eyes up, or their pockets.

No drums to stun their Mother's ear,
Nor swords to make their sisters fear;
But pretty books to store their mind
With knowledge of each various kind.

But where I found the children naughty,
In manners rude, in temper haughty,
Thankless to parents, liars, swearers,
Boxers, or cheats, or base tale-bearers,

I left a long, black, birchen rod,
Such as the dread command of God
Directs a Parent's hand to use
When virtue's path his sons refuse.

Santa brought gifts to good girls and boys, but he also carried a birch rod. Santa's thin wagon was pulled by a single reindeer—but both driver and team would get a major overhaul the next year.

The most important literature for the basis of the modern-day version of Santa Claus comes from the Christmas poem "A Visit From St. Nicholas" by Clement C. Moore. For the first time, a complete description of Santa Claus was given so children of all ages could picture him in their minds and look for him in the sky. In the poem, Moore conjured up an elfin man with a sleigh guided by eight miniature reindeer. They fly him from rooftop to rooftop and at each residence he comes down the chimney to fill stockings hung by the fireplace with gifts.[11]

Moore had written the poem for the enjoyment of his own family, but in 1823 it was published anonymously in the *Troy Sentinel*. It became epically popular and has been reprinted countless times under the more familiar title, "The Night Before Christmas." [12] The poem sustains the image of the plump, jolly Santa described therein who rides a sleigh driven by eight well-loved reindeer. The poem is still a part of Christmas tradition in America nearly two centuries later.

Eight tiny reindeer

[11] History.com editors. "Santa Claus". (2018, December 6). Retrieved from https://www.history.com/topics/christmas/santa-claus

[12] Handwerk, Brian. "From St. Nicholas to Santa Claus: The Surprising Origins of Kris Kringle". (2018, December 25). Retrieved from https://www.nationalgeographic.com/news/2018/12/131219-santa-claus-origin-history-christmas-facts-st-nicholas/

THE MAN BEHIND THE BEARD

"A Visit From Saint Nicholas"

'Twas the night before Christmas, when all through the house
Not a creature was stirring, not even a mouse;
The stockings were hung by the chimney with care,
In hopes that St. Nicholas soon would be there;

The children were nestled all snug in their beds,
While visions of sugar-plums danced in their heads;
And mamma in her 'kerchief, and I in my cap,
Had just settled down for a long winter's nap,

When out on the lawn there arose such a clatter,
I sprang from the bed to see what was the matter.
Away to the window I flew like a flash,
Tore open the shutters and threw up the sash.

The moon on the breast of the new-fallen snow
Gave the lustre of mid-day to objects below.
When, what to my wondering eyes should appear,
But a miniature sleigh, and eight tiny reindeer,

With a little old driver, so lively and quick,
I knew in a moment it must be St. Nick.
More rapid than eagles his coursers they came,
And he whistled, and shouted, and called them by name;

SANTA CLAUS' INTRODUCTION

Now, Dasher! Now, Dancer! Now, Prancer and Vixen!
On, Comet! On Cupid! On, Donder and Blitzen!
To the top of the porch! To the top of the wall!
Now dash away! Dash away! Dash away all!

As dry leaves that before the wild hurricane fly,
When they meet with an obstacle, mount to the sky,
So up to the house-top the coursers they flew,
With the sleigh full of toys, and St. Nicholas too.

And then, in a twinkling, I heard on the roof
The prancing and pawing of each little hoof.
As I drew in my hand, and was turning around,
Down the chimney St. Nicholas came with a bound.

He was dressed all in fur, from his head to his foot,
And his clothes were all tarnished with ashes and soot;
A bundle of toys he had flung on his back,
And he looked like a peddler just opening his pack.

His eyes -- how they twinkled! His dimples how merry!
His cheeks were like roses, his nose like a cherry!
His droll little mouth was drawn up like a bow,
And the beard of his chin was as white as the snow;

THE MAN BEHIND THE BEARD

The stump of a pipe he held tight in his teeth,

And the smoke it encircled his head like a wreath;

He had a broad face and a little round belly,

That shook, when he laughed like a bowlful of jelly.

He was chubby and plump, a right jolly old elf,

And I laughed when I saw him, in spite of myself;

A wink of his eye and a twist of his head,

Soon gave me to know I had nothing to dread;

He spoke not a word, but went straight to his work,

And filled all the stockings; then turned with a jerk,

And laying his finger aside of his nose,

And giving a nod, up the chimney he rose;

He sprang to his sleigh, to his team gave a whistle,

And away they all flew like the down of a thistle.

But I heard him exclaim, ere he drove out of sight,

"Happy Christmas to all, and to all a good-night!"

Santa morphed from a "jolly old elf" who drove a "miniature sleigh" guided by "eight tiny reindeer" into an ever-evolving figure in American culture.

St. Nicholas' evolution continued through the late 19th century. He developed into Santa Claus, a full-sized adult, dressed in a handsome red and white suit, who lives at the North Pole, travels around the globe on Christmas Eve in a reindeer-driven sleigh, and ultimately ensures that children behave.[13]

Thomas Nast, the great political cartoonist, was central to creating the grandfatherly, kind figure that children have grown to recognize and love. Nast provided Saint Nicholas with a workshop for making toys in the North Pole and a list of good and bad children to consult before gifts were delivered. Still, Santa's look was not yet complete with Nast's version.

Thomas Nast Santa Claus

By the mid-nineteenth century, savvy marketers realized the attraction of Santa Claus for their shoppers. Offering a glimpse at a life-sized Santa attracted thousands of children to a Philadelphia shop. Quickly shopkeepers figured out that the only thing better than a model Santa Claus was a real live one! Santa Claus was linked to shopping forevermore![14]

James Edgar, a businessman in Brockton, Massachusetts, became the first department store Santa in 1890. Understanding children's desire to see and be seen by Santa Claus, Edgar devised the plan to

---

[13] Handwerk, Brian. "From St. Nicholas to Santa Claus: The Surprising Origins of Kris Kringle". (2018, December 25). Retrieved from https://www.nationalgeographic.com/news/2018/12/131219-santa-claus-origin-history-christmas-facts-st-nicholas/

[14] History.com editors. "Santa Claus". (2018, December 6). Retrieved from https://www.history.com/topics/christmas/santa-claus

have Santa at the store for children to talk to and ask for gifts. His plan worked! From far and wide children harassed their parents until they took them to Edgar's store to see Santa Claus. Other businesses were soon to follow suit.[15]

Even magazine editors realized the popularity of St. Nicholas/Santa Claus. *St. Nicholas Magazine* was a popular monthly American children's magazine founded by Scribner's in 1873. The first editor was Mary Mapes Dodge who continued her association with the magazine until her death in 1905. Dodge published work by the country's best writers, including Louisa May Alcott of *Little Women* fame.[16]

[15] The Week staff. "The History of Santa Claus: 7 Interesting Facts" (2011, December 23). Retrieved from https://theweek.com/articles/479681/history-santa-claus-7-interesting-facts

[16] The Editors of Encyclopedia Britannica. "Mary Mapes Dodge: American Author" (2019, August 17).

In the first issue, Dodge explained why she chose St. Nicholas for the name of the magazine:

"Is he not the boys' and girls' own Saint, the especial friend of young Americans?... And what is more, isn't he the kindest, best, and jolliest old dear that ever was known?... He has attended so many heart-warmings in his long, long day that he glows without knowing it, and, coming as he does, at a holy time, casts a light upon the children's faces that lasts from year to year.... Never to dim this light, young friends, by word or token, to make it even brighter, when we can, in good, pleasant helpful ways, and to clear away clouds that sometimes shut it out, is our aim and prayer."[17]

Near the turn of the twentieth century, the Salvation Army needed a new source of monies to fund the free Christmas meals they provided to needy families. Calling upon the good-nature of people and their reaction to a charitable icon, the Salvation Army began dressing up unemployed men in Santa Claus suits and sending them into the streets of New York to request donations. Those Salvation Army Santas have been ringing bells on the street corners of American cities ever since.[18]

Santa became a full-sized advertiser in the 20th Century. His power to market and move merchandise in the modern world made him a hot pitch-man. Coca-Cola® solidified Santa's image in 1931 when they used him in their advertising campaign.

---

[17] Dodge, Mary Mapes. "Introduction", St. Nicholas: Scribner's Illustrated Magazine For Girls and Boys. (1873, November).

[18] History.com editors. "Santa Claus". (2018, December 6). Retrieved from https://www.history.com/topics/christmas/santa-claus

Coca-Cola® commissioned Michigan-born illustrator Haddon Sundblom to develop advertising images using Santa Claus, who was to be both realistic as a man unto himself and symbolic at the same time.

For inspiration, Sundblom turned to Clement Clark Moore's 1822 poem "A Visit From St. Nicholas." Moore's description of St. Nicholas led to an image of a kind, non-threatening, full-bellied Santa.

Sundblom's Santa debuted in 1931 in Coke ads in *The Saturday Evening Post* and appeared regularly in that magazine, as well as in many other popular magazines of the day.

From 1931 to 1964, Coca-Cola® advertising showed Santa in myriad scenes, usually a Coke in hand, in all of the ways children envisioned him. From reading a child's letter to playing with toys, Sundblom captured the imagination of children, young and old. His Coca-Cola® Santa Claus became the bar which still exists today. Sundblom's original paintings became the basis of the Coca-Cola® advertising in magazines and several other pieces of merchandise like calendars and posters. Many of those items today are popular collectibles.[19]

Sundblom's images replaced many others in the minds and hearts of Americans.

In more recent times, in Colorado, there is a Santa Claus University that teaches people how to become professional Santas.

---

[19] Conversations staff. "5 Things You Never Knew About Santa Claus and Coca-Cola". (2012, January 1). Retrieved from https://www.coca-colacompany.com/stories/coke-lore-santa-claus

Strict adhesion to the program is essential to success. To become a graduate, one must take courses including posing for pictures, proper ways to dress, beard sculpting and maintenance, and more.[20]

But not all who don the Santa Claus suit and take on his personality have been formally trained at Santa Claus University. Some, like Pat Ficcio, came to become Santa Claus via a different path. His calling, strong, his dedication, complete. This is Pat's story.

---

[20] DeRousse, Edmond P. "St. Nicholas/Santa Clause Some History". (2018, December 17). Retrieved from https://www.commonmanadventures.com/st-nicholas-santa-clause-some-history/

INTRODUCING PAT FICCIO

Six months before Haddon Sundblom's Coca Cola Santa was put into advertisements, a baby was born in Newark, NJ.

Pasquale Ficcio – Pat – was born on June 12, 1931 to Carmine and Teresa. Carmine was born in Calabritto, an Italian town in the province of Avellino, Campania, Italy. It occupies a hilly-mountainous area at the eastern tip of the Monti Picentini range. At 17, he left Calabritto for the United States via Ellis Island. Carmine's sister had also immigrated to America, but her journey took her to Philadelphia

Pat's parents

instead. Carmine settled in the Italian section of Newark, NJ where he met and eventually married Teresa Sierchio. Teresa was an Italian American whose parents were born in Italy.

Before Pasquale arrived, his parents had two daughters. Pat was born at his parents' home by midwife and weighed in at nearly 14 pounds! Pat recalls stories of his sisters looking at him sitting on the family's kitchen table when they arrived home on the day of his birth. "Look what Mama brought you," they were told.

Jane with Pat at his Christening

Pat was surround by family, food, faith, and love in his formative years. He recalls vividly Sunday family dinners, extended family in many of his memories, and the Church being the center of his world when it wasn't the family kitchen.

Pat's mother was a great cook. She made the family meals and certainly taught Pat, an avid cook himself, the basics of working in the kitchen. He describes numerous dishes that would be sprawled across the table when family gathered. "But I don't recall my mother being a baker," Pat said. "My grandmother was the baker. She would make the most amazing things." Pat, too, was taught by his grandmother so, he, too, is a marvel at baking.

What Pat does recall lovingly about time with his mother revolves around steps that wound outside the window where his mother would sew. Pat would climb the steps and perch outside his mother's sewing window to talk to her. He'd have a sandwich on Italian bread, split and filled with

Pat as a toddler c.1932

peanut butter and bananas. There he would talk to his mother, a fact that doesn't escape Pat's appreciation for his life. "If it wasn't for that staircase in that exact location, I probably wouldn't have spent that time with my mother."

Pat does recall spending a lot of time with his dad growing up. They would go to Newark's beautiful Branch Brook Park. Pat, like many he knew in Newark, lived in a multi-generational home. On his mother's side, Pat's Grandmother and Grandfather lived upstairs, their children – Pat's Aunts and Uncles – lived in the home, too. Pat's Mom and Dad had a room, and Pat and his sisters slept together when he was a little boy. Once he got older, he shared rooms with his uncles.

Michael Angelo & Giovanni Sierchio, Pat's maternal grandparents with whom he lived

"Everyone lived and everyone visited, our front door was never locked." Pat shared. "People just rang the bell and came right in. That was in Newark, a great place to grow up when I was a child."

Regarding his youth, Pat has vivid memories sleeping downstairs in the living room of his home and being awakened by the horse drawn carriage delivering the milk. The milkman would take his six to eight bottles of milk to the various homes as the horse would continue down the road a piece. Once the milkman returned to the carriage to reload his deliveries by hand and set off by foot again, the horse would again go down the street driverless. He knew the route so well that he could progress down the street in a routine that he and the milkman had developed. Pat heard the tinkling of milk bottles as the horse slowly went up the street. It is a memory emblazoned on Pat's brain because he thinks of these memories with the same joy and happiness that colors all of his life.

"I remember the Rag man. He came by in a horse and buggy and buy newspapers and scraps from you. He would have his scale. He would weigh your papers and rags and pay you for them by the pound. He'd say, 'Rags, Rags!' and people would come out to sell their scraps and newspapers. This is what they would do to make a little extra money from the Rag man. That's the way I grew up in my life. I remember these things so vividly, and I want to share these memories because they're precious to me and perhaps make others remember."

Cars existed then, but this was the way business was conducted when Pat was a child in Newark. Pat even recalls that Dugan Bakery had a battery-operated truck that ran silently!

"During the war (WWII), there were air raids. The neighborhood went dark, people were silent. It was about 1941 and it made a deep impression on me. It was a part of my life. "

"My grandmother's two sons were in the military. One of my uncles was in Pearl Harbor and survived the war and lived until he was 95 years old. He treated me like I was his own son. We lived together, of course, until he got married."

Pat was sent to Catholic school where he was a decent student with many friends. His good temperament, lust for life, and connecting with humanity served him well throughout Pat's childhood. Even his lovely voice keeps Pat connected to his Church.

"I love singing, I just love singing. When I'm in Church, I sing because I just love it. And I know most of the hymns because when I was a child, I was in the choir. So, I'm going back to the choir again. Who knew that I would be going back to the choir?" Pat refers to returning to the choir after a decades-long absence. He became a member again in October 2018.

"You have to feel what you sing. You have to see what you sing. Dad sang "Silent Night" in July!" Pat remembers clearly.

In December 2018, Pat and his fellow Men's Choir members went out to dinner. There, the men broke out into song, and Pat had presence of mind to record it on his phone. The 14 men who were assembled at the table sang "Silent Night" for themselves and everyone in the restaurant. It was mesmerizing. It wasn't lost on Pat that the song is the one his father always sang to him.

Halloween was a memorable time for Pat. "I used to go get my brown paper bag, fill it up, go home, empty it, and then go out again!"

Pat instantly recalls a bakery on Orange Street in Newark called Braun's. They made a cinnamon brown cupcake with chocolate icing on it, like a spice cupcake. Pat's mouth waters describing its sugary, tasty goodness.

"We would have to walk through the hallway, go in through a door, they'd stamp your hand, we'd put Vaseline on our hands. We would wait a few minutes, rub off the stamp, and go through again. 'Weren't you already here young man?'"

"Must have been my twin brother!" Pat's quick wit retorted.

"Until today, I still love that cupcake. Nutley bakery makes one similar to the one Braun's used to make."

Trick-or-Treating took place on the main street in Newark which is Orange Street.

"We would make our costumes - get charcoal and put it on our face. Get a $1.98 costume. At homes where we trick-or-treated, we got cookies, apples, basic foods, not wrapped candy, little bags of candy corn, simple things, and maybe raisins. Pennies, too."

"In Chatham, I would give out pennies, nickels, and dimes. A few neighborhood kids would get a dollar. There would be eight to ten kids at a clip, then they'd leave, and another group would come. "Hey, they're giving money at this house!"

Decorations were not elaborate for Halloween. Pat would get a pumpkin and put it on the porch. Squirrels would come and attack it.

Thanksgiving was the true start of the holiday season. The Thanksgiving Day Parade in the morning in Newark with Santa bringing up the rear and ending at Bambergers started the day's festivities.

From 7th Avenue to Roseville Avenue to the Armory to West Market Street to Bambergers was the route.

Men went to the parade and the women stayed home to cook.

Although an avid cook today, Pat remembers, "I was out playing with the kids outside, with my uncles."

Dinner was an Italian American celebration. It would consist of the following: antipasto, soup, pasta, turkey.

Camille laments that in her home growing up, "Nobody would have room for turkey after eating all day long. The turkey was served around eight o'clock at night."

Pat responds in earnest, "I don't know about you, but I had room!"

While reminiscing about their respective Thanksgiving spread, the menu looked like the following:

Sweet potatoes (sweet potato pie for Camille)

Artichokes stuffed with breadcrumbs, garlic, parsley, pignoli (pine nuts), butter (Camille)

Turkey stuffed with chestnuts

Breast of veal (Pat)

"Camille's sister-in-law doesn't cook the turkey, she crucifies it!" Pat says wickedly.

Mashed potatoes prepared with cherry peppers, cut up - take out the seeds - a little garlic cooked up (not browned) put whole mixture into the potatoes.

Stuffed veal - open the pocket with egg and sausage and garlic and bread

"I ate turkey more later in my life with my sisters," Pat admits.

Christmas was important in his Catholic family. Pat recalls the entire season and how it always began in early December when a cousin would come calling on his family. "My cousin, Marie, would come to the door, and my sisters and I would be so excited. She would always bring the beautiful ribbon hard candies so elegantly wrapped. I just loved that candy! My mother would hide the candy high up on the mantle of the fireplace, away from little hands."

Pat and his sisters were allowed to sleep in the living room on a pull-out bed. There was a mantel above the fireplace where Pat's mother placed the candy. Determinedly, Pat found ways to climb and get his little hands on that box of delectable candy. He ate a lot and put other pieces in his pocket. One time he ate so much of it after snagging it out of its hiding place, he got a bellyache! His eyes sparkle as he remembers the feel and taste of the seasonal treat.

Approximately a week before Christmas, Pat and his family would buy a cut tree to bring into their home to decorate. "I

Pat's mom, dad, and sister, Jean, seated next to the family Christmas tree. Note the beautiful creche with the Nativity scene. December 25, 1957

remember so vividly setting the tree up at Christmas then the Nativity scene we'd set up."

Ornaments would be festooned on the tree. Treasures from dime stores, shaped in all different manners, lay delicately in the branches. Pat remembers one that was a banana! They were small pieces of art that he recalls with adoration.

Always laying under the Tannenbaum was the family's crèche made by Carmine with Nativity scene. The Holy Family, the Three Wise Men, and the Barn Animals.

"The sheep had the thinnest, spindly legs, like toothpicks!" He still speaks of them with awe. A search has been conducted by Pat to find those original pieces.

As with much of Pat's childhood, Christmas was marked by family visiting and creating a huge meal for all to share. On Christmas Eve, the feast to enjoy was The Feast of the Seven Fishes, a traditional seafood fare for many Italian Americans.

Eating fish on Christmas Eve is a tradition that stems from the Roman Catholic custom of abstinence from meat and dairy products on the eve of certain holidays, including Christmas. The number seven was vastly important throughout Christian history: in fact, seven is written more than 700 times in the Bible. In the Roman Catholic Church, seven are the sacraments, the days of the Creation, as well as the deadly sins. So seven courses were inevitable for the Christmas Eve meal.

In the early 20th Century, Italian-American families, longing to connect to the Old World and their traditions, began preparing "The Feast of the Seven Fishes." An homage to their Italian heritage, this menu was truly an American creation that has become a wonderful tradition.

After Christmas Eve dinner, Pat and his family would walk to Midnight Mass at St. Lucy's Church. His eyes dance and twinkle recalling the beauty of the church on that night. Pat sang in the choir and he loved that so much. Simply being in church, then being honored to sing in church, filled Pat with great feelings of love and pride.

It would be very late after church services. The family would return home. They might eat some more sausage and peppers because Christmas Eve had finally transitioned to Christmas Day, and meat was allowed to be consumed again, but eventually the house would fall silent as they all settled their heads to rest before Christmas morning.

If they didn't go to church Christmas Eve, they'd go on Christmas Day.

Pat knows well that Santa Claus always visited his home. There would be a few gifts near the tree, but not too close as to disrupt the Nativity scene in the crèche. And, Santa Claus always put surprises in Pat's stocking that hung on the mantle.

"Inside my stocking was always a piece of fruit, candies, perhaps a foil-wrapped chocolate Santa, and a little toy like jacks or marbles."

"I liked candies, and I still do!" Pat says with a smile on his lips.

"I loved marbles. I used to wear knickers, and I had a hole in my pocket that went down to the knickers. We used to play on a patch of dirt outside of the house. I was the marble shark on the street. When I would come home, I would be there all day playing marbles. Like a pool table we had so many holes. You had to do hole 1, 2, 3, 4 etc. If somebody was ahead of you, you just knocked them out of the way!"

"We sent my son, Tom, all of my marbles and he has them proudly displayed in a jar."

"Sometimes we'd get cards, like baseball cards. We used those to play a card game where we flipped the cards down the wall. It was a competition. We would try to make our cards land on the cards that were there before our turn. If our card landed on someone else's, we'd get to keep the cards."

"My favorite baseball team was the Yankees and still is!"

And, there were times when Pat found himself in a bit of trouble. He'd hit a ball or "an article" through a window and it would go "clink clink clink and we ran for the hills!"

"Whose window did you break?!" Pat's mother asked. Because the neighbors told her, "Your son was playing and broke things!"

"My grandfather was a carpenter by trade, I had to go with him to the hardware. He'd measure the glass what he had to get, got the tools to hold it and the putty. I had to scrape the old glass out, put the new glass in, and then place the glass with the putty. My grandfather was there to supervise and make sure I didn't get hurt. But he made me do it."

"I never wanted to become a carpenter or a painter like my dad. My dad was an artist, not just a painter. He used to paint expertly on a fresh, clean, plain wall and create the look of marble, wood, or tile. He'd painstakingly use his tools – quality paintbrushes he brought over from Italy when he was 17 years old – to create the look of marble on the blank canvas of the wall. He'd envision a piece of marble and recreate it with rich color, variations, and veins he'd etched from his fingernail. If my dad was painting a door or wall that was to look like wood, he'd miraculously create the wood's grain including knots from his paintbrush. His calling was painting. His talent was undeniable. I used to love watching my dad work. His creative process was mesmerizing. My dad didn't promote his work, but he was always requested to do jobs."

"My dad would be sitting in the backyard. My dad left me with such a feeling. I'd watch him. He did things that made me really respect him. He would buy the Italian paper and read the Italian paper. Then, he would buy the Newark Star Ledger, and he'd read it from pictures, then a few words, and he taught himself to read English. He'd sit out in the backyard in a shirt and tie and read the paper. Always a gentleman. I looked up to him because he was my dad."

"As a young boy we went sleigh riding at Branch Brook Park on the weekends. My father would come with us, and he'd stay on top of the hill until we convinced him to come down the hill with us. Many times he would get stuck on the sleigh, and his face would go in the snow! It was a fun thing. It would be bitter cold, but we weren't cold. We were loaded with families there. Two and a half blocks from where we live, over the bridge near where the city subway ran (and still runs but the bridge is gone). There were dozens of kids."

"A sled was something one would have asked for at Christmas. A Flexible Flyer. We'd pack the snow down, make it slick, we'd fly down the hill. We tried to see who was getting closest to the lake, although we weren't in danger of going in, just to see who could get closest. I was usually rosy cheeked and cold."

"It was a simpler time. I think anything that we DID do was a special thing. We never took anything for granted. It was 'I get to do this' not 'I have to do this.'"

"Life is Beautiful," Pat says with a gleam in his eye and his contagious smile.

Gifts were never the most important part of the day to Pat whose childhood coincided with America's Great Depression. Pat has the sense of gifts being given for the holiday, "And I thought 'Wow!'", but it always was about the family, the food, and the Church to him.

"I just love living these memories over and over."

Mom made ravioli. While Grandma sewed, Pat would get two pieces of Italian bread, spread it with peanut butter on both sides of the bread, and add sliced banana with a quart of milk.

Pat always felt, "Santa and I had something in common. Why? I don't know why, but it seems that when I was born it was 1931 and, not realizing it, that was the same year the Newark Bamberger's parade started."

"When I was a year or two years old, my dad would take me to the Thanksgiving Day Parade right down the street because we had some floats which were at the end of our block. They would go up 7th Avenue to Roseville Avenue where the Armory was, meet up with the other floats, and then march on down to Newark."

"My dad took me and put me on his shoulder and took me to the end of the block. I remember the Clydesdale horses which impressed me."

"Then, of course, I didn't see Santa Claus because he wasn't in our particular area, and I got to see him on West Market Street. My dad would take me from where we lived, right across three, four, or five blocks to West Market Street which is where the parade route was and where I got to see Santa which excited me again. And, we wouldn't go down to Bamberger's that day because we got to see the parade."

When Pat saw Santa Claus as a little boy at Bamberger's he was always thrilled. "I asked Santa for a lot of things back then!" Pausing for a moment, Pat states emphatically, "I feel now that, now that I've been doing Santa for the number of years that I have, I really felt that maybe I was meant to do this. I feel it had to be a calling, because why am I doing it now over 70 years?"

"For me to continue to do it, I feel it's something that is so special. It never bothered me to put on the suit. I always look forward to playing Santa, I'd always get excited in September knowing in December I'd get to play Santa Claus."

In a deep voice Camille says, "Is my suit ready?" to which Pat laughs knowingly in agreement.

"Just being a child I had that desire to go downtown and see Santa in Newark. I always felt great excitement and I still do today after all of these years being Santa."

What Pat continues to do year in, and year out began in December 1948, a date when Pat Ficcio's life changed forever. As a 17 year old high school student at St. Michael's School in Newark, NJ, Pat was selected among his classmates to play Santa Claus for a Christmas play performed at the school. "Everyone else was playing elves, and since I was the chubby one, I volunteered to be Santa."

Rose Toma & Pat
St. Michael's High
School, Newark, NJ
Dec. 22, 1948

Active in his church, Pat reveled in playing Santa for the children who attended Saturday movies there. He and his friends filled a wagon top to look like a sleigh. Pat's friends, two of whom were dressed like elves, pulled him into the hall where the children were. There Pat gave the children candy. One little boy was so moved he gave Pat two pennies!

As time marched on, Pat received more requests to play Santa.

Except for a stint in the Army when he was stationed in Germany in the early 1950's, Pat has been Santa Claus for over 70 years. "Every year I just look forward to doing it. Christmas is a time for children to be happy and what better way to make them smile?"

Pat as Santa Claus for the first time with his "elves." St. Michael's High School, Newark, NJ - Dec. 22, 1948

While in the service, Pat, stationed in Germany, was able to take a trip to Italy to visit the place his father had lived. He wrote to his father to tell him the plan. Pat and a couple of buddies went to Italy, got on a bus in Salerno, and traveled to Calabritto in the mountains. When the men finally arrived, Pat said it was like a dignitary was among them. The entire town had come out and welcomed the bus with an extravaganza. The only people getting off the bus were Pat and his friends. Obviously, Pat's father had wired ahead of Pat's

Pat in Germany Oct. 1950

35

visit, and the townsfolk were ecstatic to meet their kin from America.

Immediately Pat was met by his namesake uncle, Pasquale. Then, a nun took Pat by the hand to show him something extraordinary. It was a type of daycare set up in the nunnery to care for the children of the townsfolk who had to work. The money Pat's father had sent over regularly from the States had helped to fund this all-important care center for the children of Calabritto.

For Pat, this trip to the Old World was special for myriad reasons. First, Pat's father Carmine was a wonderful artist. Hanging in Pat's home was a beautiful mural of Calabritto. It was a scene Pat had

Army buddy, Bob, with Pat having a beer on Christmas Day with their German friends

grown up looking at his entire life. When he looked outside the bus for the first time, Pat knew he was in Calabritto because, "It looked exactly the way my dad had painted it."

Secondly, Pat was welcomed like a hero in his father's hometown. Being Carmine Ficcio's son made him an immediate hometown hero. Everybody came to greet Pat and his friends. And, when Pat fished out his camera to memorialize the day, every child in town crowded into the picture to be captured for the momentous occasion.

One of the grateful townsfolk, Gerardo, told Pat, "You American soldiers are just remarkable. We were bombed out during the war, but you American soldiers came through the area. We had no food, and you gave it to us. We needed clothes, and you provided them for us in the village."

Villagers of Calabritto, Italy posing for the pictures c. 1953

Lastly, seeing the day care center his father helped fund was very touching for Pat. It drove home the point that the Ficcio Family was a family that gave of their time, money, and service. More importantly, they did it for children.

Carmine, inspired by his son's trip, returned to his hometown in 1956. And like Carmine, Calabritto became a part of Pat. He can still smell, taste, and see it in his mind's eye, and he carries it with him to this day.

During the years serving his country, Pat was ever-forming his Santa Claus persona and his dedication to making children happy.

Over the years, Pat's role as Santa Claus has been as personal as dressing up at his place of work annually to surprise his co-workers and to hand out gifts to dressing up at his home to make his son's Christmas wondrous.

Early on, Pat used to rent his Santa suit, but it quickly became evident that buying a suit was the right thing to do as his role as Santa kept expanding.

When Pat was recruited to play Santa at his child's great-grandma's home, he jumped at the chance. His son and all of his cousins gathered there, and Pat was to surprise them all. The only child who cried was Pat's son. His cousin, Judith, told him not to cry as Santa was actually his father, then she made him promise not to tell the other children who were wide-eyed in their belief.

The Carmine Ficcio Family from l to r: Mary (sister), Mom, Jean (sister), Dad, and Pat

In addition to the children in his family, Pat would don the Santa suit to pay visits to all of his friends and relatives. He would bring gifts and good cheer wherever he went. From scrumptious boxes filled with panettone to exquisite bone-china made by Lenox, Pat has generously surprised loved-ones with his thoughtful gifts.

"I was bringing smiles to everyone I would see and who would see me. I began to see it was a thing I had to do every Christmas, not just for the children, but for everyone."

"There was a Christmas when my mom and dad lived in Bellville with my sister, Jean. Claire, Tom, and I went there and were shocked to see there was no Christmas tree."

"Where's your tree?" Pat asked.

They replied they'd had no time to get one and set it up.

"Jean, it's Christmas! You can't have Christmas without a tree!" Pat ordered.

Tom, who was a teenager, and Pat went out to get a tree from a vendor on Route 10. No one was out selling trees anymore on Christmas Eve. At a gas station, Tom and Pat saw some Christmas trees. Pat asked Tom to see who was around. When no one could be found, Tom quipped to his father, "Are you going to sell it to me, or am I going to sell it to you?"

With no one around, Tom asked his dad, "How do you like this tree?"

"That tree looks good," Pat agreed.

The men took the tree home to Pat's parents' home in Bellville. They didn't feel like thieves.

Upon returning to the family's home, Pat and Tom opened the door with the Christmas tree. Pat announced, "Jean, get out the ornaments, your tree needs to be decorated!" Pat remembers vividly how his mom and dad's eyes were gleaming.

"I felt the spirit of Christmas was for anyone who believed and that made it happen. I had to share that gift with everyone."

"My life as Santa was my gift, I had to share with everyone."

Pat has taken his role from chocolate stores to grocery stores, hospitals to nursing homes, club houses to neighbor visits, and schools.

"My love of for children and people made my role as Santa very easy to portray."

"When we left Chatham (NJ), the neighbors put out two chairs on the driveway for Pat and Camille. They sat and all of the children in the neighborhood came by and wished them well."

Each visit, each year that rolls by, leaves Pat more excited to be Santa than the last. He never tires of the travel, the costume donning, the appearances, the lap time, or the delight he gets from talking to children of all ages.

Over the years, Pat has accumulated thousands of memories, mementos, and accounts of his time as Santa Claus. He is so humbled and proud to be able to share his lifelong message of peace, happiness, excitement, and joy in this book.

"I guess I looked at Santa as...my part as Santa Claus is what the children see as Santa Claus."

"Are you a mirror back to what they need to see?"

"Yes. And I love speaking to the children. That to me is so important. I just can't see having a child coming up and getting a gift from me. I have to speak to them a little bit."

"I've done it in so many different areas, different sections, different people, and I look forward to going to my relatives and friends to give gifts. I'd go over to my favorite place in Totowa, Thomas' which had a distribution place, and we would buy 15-20 panettone. I would deliver them to my family and friends at Christmas time. I used to bring candy to work and a piece of Lennox for the girls at work, at Christmas time they all got one. I did it for Camille's club members. They would be wrapped up, a Christmas gift from Santa. To me, it's the gift of giving, it was just the pleasures I had of doing that. Giving. That joy. That's why I enjoy doing it so much. I get so excited at Christmas time."

TOM FICCIO

Tom was the only child of Pat and his wife Claire Luchko. Claire was Pat's high school sweetheart. She was from the North Newark section and would never have crossed her path had he not met Claire at school. The courtship began almost immediately upon meeting. The two double dated with another couple from school. The popular spot of the day was Keansburg where there used to be an amusement park. Pat, Claire, their good friends and two other couples, four couples total, went there for fun and recreation.

Pat and Claire became engaged before Pat went to service. They wrote many letters to one another. Their courtship resulted in the couple's marriage in 1954.

"She never got into the Santa Claus bit." Pat states matter-of-factly. "She enjoyed it; Claire used to come with me."

When asked directly why Claire wasn't the Mrs. to his Santa Claus Pat quipped, "She didn't play Mrs. Claus because she didn't have white hair!"

But Pat relayed that Claire was an active woman who "belonged to the Rosary Society at Church. I used to be Santa for different events with the school."

The couple's only child, son Tom, was born in 1956.

The little family lived in Newark, but Pat worked in Summit, NJ, a town not far from Chatham. During the riots in Newark, Pat decided he had to do something to ensure his family's safety. "Before it got too bad, I decided to relocate my family to Chatham."

Pat and Claire wanted only the best for their son. "I wanted Tom to enjoy his childhood life as much as I did mine."

And, because family is so vastly important to Pat, he made sure Tom was exposed to family on both his side and Claire's.

Claire's grandparents were Slovak and were located in Dunmore, PA outside of Scranton.

Tom's childhood was marked with myriad visits to the family homestead. He loved it with wild abandon.

"Dad, this is fun, I can go in the back door and come out the front because they're not locked!" an impressed Tom told his father. Living in the city of Newark, no door remained unlocked in Tom's world, until he came to his maternal grandparents' home in the country.

Claire's grandparents/Tom's great-grandparents in Pennsylvania

In addition to Claire's family, "We did a lot with my local family with Tom," Pat tells.

"He loved Grandma here in New Jersey, but he also loved Grandma in Pennsylvania."

In PA, "He (Tom) loved to eat the traditional food they had like kielbasa and pierogi, kolach – rolled dough with poppy seed spread inside – beets, and a handmade cheese ball."

Camille adds, "We got Donna (Tom's wife) a book with traditional Slovak recipes. She's wonderful and makes all of these authentic recipes for Tom."

Tom got to know both sides of his family. He played cards – hearts or something like that.

Each year, Tom would visit with his mother's younger sister, his Aunt Lorraine. She was married to a military man, but wherever they were, Virginia for example, Pat, Claire, and Tom would make a visit annually. Consequently, Tom was and is very close to his cousins.

Growing up, Tom was involved in Little League, so Pat decided to be the coach. He was excellent at cheering his players on who had all different levels and temperaments. In his capacity as coach, Pat once again championed the children who needed him most. In one case, a boy on the Chatham team was acting out terribly and not showing up where he needed to be on the field. When questioned, the boy stated he was looking for his father who was often absent from practice and games. Pat reasoned, "Well, I gotta become a Dad for him. I have to be the Dad his would have been if he had the tools to do it himself."

Pat was firm yet loving. He used reason and never raised his temper to a child. Camille confirms this fact. Pat melts these situations with his calm and psychology "and I get so much more out of them when I treat them that way."

Pat is a mentor to children, not just as a Santa Claus, but in life. It's another factor that showcases his dedication to children.

Like Pat, Tom adores Christmas. Tom collects Department 56 and lovingly sets them up each holiday season.

Tom and Donna Ficcio's Christmas Village display

And, although Tom loves Christmas, he's never donned the Santa Suit. It doesn't diminish how proud he is of his father. In fact, he's thrilled with Pat. The relationship the two men share is a beautiful thing.

"We've done Santa Claus together like when he bowled with the children in Chatham, he'd drive up with me dressed as Santa because he knew who Santa Claus was, of course. He would run in

Tom with his dad Pat

first to make sure the children didn't know who Santa was. He was in on it, but never wanted to spoil the magic for the other children."

"I used to take so many pictures with children but never got the pictures from the parents. That's the thing that I miss so much, so dearly."

Tom with wife, Donna and his dad, Pat

Camille added, "And we didn't really know the people."

Imagine how many photo albums Pat and Camille are featured.

"Why am I still doing it? The love that I have for Santa. For the children. What joy I bring to the children, the seniors, and everyone."

SANTA CLAUS COLLECTION

We all know people who collect things. Maybe grandma collected teacups, dad collects Matchbox® cars, and perhaps you know a neighbor who collects cats. But, did you know Santa loves to collect things, too? It's true. Pat loves to collect a new Santa toy or figure each year. He has accumulated quite a vast and interesting collection.

"I remember so vividly setting the tree up at Christmas then the Nativity scene we'd set up."

"One side of the storage is just Christmas. If I ever took it out and put everything on display it would be a Christmas Wonderland!"

Pat recalls, "Every time I saw something new pertaining to Christmas, I would buy it. I have Santas, Angels. Whatever it is, it's got to speak to me. I have two bears playing banjos that sit on a rail fence and they play together. I get at least one (Christmas item) a year, at least. I gave a lot to my son, I guess, he took some stuff with him. But I don't want to part with it."

His favorite is a figure of a praying Santa placed between two green candles.

Pat and Camille's home is decorated with Santa and Mrs. Claus dangling from the lamp post as well as the Nativity Scene.

There is a gorgeous tree with reliefs of the Holy Family, a Nativity Tree that the couple leave out year round to observe and admire.

In addition, there are four sweet angels that Pat and Camille leave out in the four corners of their living room. Each individual angel sings a lovely Christmas carol, and once one starts, the other three chime in to harmonize. They react to one another. Pat says they leave these Angels out year-round because they are too happy to put away in storage.

An article Pat read mentioned the Coca-Cola Santa collectibles of old. He was tickled to realize that he had acquired a vintage advertising truck he'd read about in the article. Coca-Cola, after all, is the reason so many Americans – and people around the world – see Santa Claus as a tall, robust, jovial, grandfatherly figure.

In the off-season, dozens of boxes of Santa Clauses in different poses line the shelves of closets in the Ficcio home. Some dance, others ski, and one is truly an Italian!

Pat prizes an ornament dated 2002 that reads "Best Friend" on a dog bone with Pat's name inscribed; a gift from a dear friend. Pat is as passionate for dogs as he is for Christmas and his role as Santa Claus.

Pat and Camille love these pieces and enjoy decorating their home with their myriad collection of Santa Clauses.

CATHOLIC CONVICTIONS

St. Gerard

Talking to Pat and Camille reveals their passion and fervor for their faith, their church, and St. Gerard. The church they attend, St. Lucy's Church in Newark, New Jersey, is the National Shrine of St. Gerard. When Pat and Camille talk to folks, and the subject of fertility, pregnancy, and birth comes up, they are quick to produce an envelope containing a letter, a handkerchief, a Novena and Prayers book with a medallion, and a warm smile to share.

Inside the envelope, a letter explains the importance of St. Gerard's Handkerchief. Here's what the letter says:

St. Gerard Handkerchief

It was toward the end of August 1755, the last year of St. Gerard's earthly life. During this time, while he was staying at Oliveto Citra in the hopes of some improvement from the serious illness which would soon end his life, Gerard visited some of the families of the town.

As he was leaving one of the homes, a young lady present there observed that he had left his handkerchief on a chair.

Thinking he had forgotten it, she picked it up, handing it to him. He, however, reading into the future, was inspired by God to say to her, "No, keep it. One day it will be of service to you." The handkerchief was the symbolic heritage that the saint left to God's creatures who have the sacred duty on earth to render, in pain, the continuation of human life.

In fact, a few years later, the young lady married. The birth of her first child was so difficult that she was at the point of death. Invoking her patron saints to deliver her appeared to be in vain until she suddenly remembered Saint Gerard's handkerchief. She asked for it and held it to herself. Not only did the pain of delivery immediately cease, but she experienced the joy of the immediate birth of her child.

Afterwards, the handkerchief was passed from one mother to another of the town as each was about to give birth, and when the first fortunate woman died, she left the precious relic to her niece. As time passed, the handkerchief was cut into so many pieces that, when the process for Gerard's canonization began, there remained only a shred of it.

The news of this miraculous handkerchief traveled farther than the borders of Oliveto Citra. Even expectant mothers who did not own a piece of handkerchief invoked this saint during hours of labor with great faith, and their prayers were not said in vain.

We know that during the beatification process in 1845, an image of Gerard was distributed bearing a reference to, and thus, making him known as the Protector of Expectant Mothers. Today, the miraculous deeds of Saint Gerard

Maiella are universally known and recognized, not only by
the faithful, but also by the authorities of the church.

Handkerchiefs which are taken to the sanctuary at
Materdomini and touched to his tomb carry blessings of the
saint to expectant mothers of the world, who, with the
protection and help of St. Gerard, experience the purest joys
of a healthy and safe delivery.

May the symbolic, blessed handkerchief of St. Gerard
help us to understand how, in these difficult times, the
beauty of maternity can become clouded by the pressures of
life. May the knowledge of it give strength to mothers to
embrace with faith and hope the Christian duties enjoined
by motherhood.

It is another way Pat and Camille revere and value motherhood
and children.

This story is one of many Pat and Camille share of how St. Gerard
works through them.

Pat and Camille were at the eye doctor, and a woman named
Eileen mentions her daughter is trying to get pregnant. Turns out
she, too, was from Newark and went to St. Rosa Lima when she was
growing up. Camille and Pat always carry the kit provided by St.
Lucy about St. Gerard.

"We have something we'd like you to have. Will you follow us up
the road?" Camille asked.

Camille came up to the condo and got the envelope with the St. Gerard information. She gave it to Eileen who was going to see her daughter over the holidays; the daughter lives in California.

Eileen said wistfully, "Maybe I'll go to church with you some day."

"We're going Sunday," Pat offered sincerely.

"I'll park at Olive Garden in Rockaway, if you don't mind picking me up," Eileen said hopefully, excitedly.

Pat and Camille picked Eileen up on that Sunday and brought her to St. Lucy's Church. She was in awe.

Eileen said, "I feel like I'm in Rome."

At the church, a permanent room downstairs has been dedicated where the collection of crèches resides.

After church, Pat and Camille drove Eileen around the old neighborhood in Newark. Eileen was overjoyed and promised to return to St. Lucy's Church.

Although Pat never made the connection fully in his head, his involvement in a unique and important project during his years as a Grand Knight serving in his Chatham parish, connects absolutely with his mission to spread the word and healing of St. Gerard.

A Legacy of Caring for Children and Their Mothers: Rose For Motherhood

"Making It One Full Basket"

Pat was always a devout and active Catholic. He credits his faith for his success as a family man, an employer, an active community member, and in his role as Santa. He's proudly served in the Knights of Columbus and speaks with pride and reverence of being a Grand Knight.

Pat becoming a Grand Knight, Parcell's Council St. Patrick's 1986

Among his many accomplishments is helping to create the Rose for Motherhood program that debuted in the mid-1980s. Roses were presented to mothers whose babies were baptized at the Sunday Masses at St. Patrick and Corpus Christi Churches. In addition to the rose, mothers were given a beautiful tribute honoring motherhood that read:

"A Rose for Motherhood"

"Parcell's Council Knights of Columbus, serving Corpus Christi Church and St. Patrick's Church, has initiated a "Rose for Motherhood" program.

"In our ongoing desire to foster the right to life, we also wish to pay tribute and honor to Motherhood. On behalf of all the members of Parcell's Council, I wish to present this rose, emblematic of love and of life, to you on this beautiful occasion. May God Bless You and Bless this New Life you have brought to our Christian Community."

Pat shares this information not only because he is proud of it – the Parcell's Council Knights of Columbus won an award for the program – but to show the dedication to children and motherhood Pat has dedicated his life.

Camille summed up Pat's focus from motherhood to children as "making it one full basket."

MAGICAL CHRISTMAS

Pat in full Santa Claus regalia calming a baby

"When Pat and I go to a store and we see a child crying, Pat goes up to the child and says, "I have to know your name. I have to tell Santa all about you. I know you are a great shopper, but why are you crying?" As the mother mouths "thank you" to Pat, the child miraculously stops crying. It's like nothing ever happens!" Camille states proudly about Pat.

"I think my life is just a gift. The gift of Life." Pat says confidently.

Pat was asked to be Santa at a Rosary Society Christmas Party. During that event he convinced the Monsignor to sit on his lap. No one could believe that he would ever do it. But, once a child, always a child; he believed. There was a Santa sharing the joy of Christmas.

On Christmas Eve after the children's mass, Pat would be at the back of the church dressed as Santa handing out candy canes to the children.

"The gift of giving was what makes my Christmas."

Meeting a child too afraid to sit on Santa's lap. Before Santa left, the child became brave and wanted to sit on Santa's lap and did.

Little boy started running toward Santa, then put the brakes on, and then ran away crying. But later, they snapped a picture with him and Santa.

At Morris View nursing home, Pat's audience was filled with sleepy, disengaged residents. He had his work cut out for him. With nary a Christmas song lyric in his

Happily sitting on Santa's lap

head, Pat took to the makeshift stage to face his lackluster audience. With God's help, a song sprang to his head. He started out in his beautiful baritone voice singing, "Let Me Call You Sweetheart." To his surprise and delight, listless forms in front of him awakened with sparkling eyes, a knowing smile, and a chorus of the song in their hearts and on their lips.

A dear friend of Pat and his wife Camille, Jo Ann, brought her 86 year old mother-in-law from Michigan to see Pat and Camille as Santa & Mrs. Claus at the Gazebo in Chatham. She had confessed to Pat that she had never sat on Santa's lap before. Pat charmed the woman and put her at ease. In her ninth decade on this good earth, Mary Lester did that day.

Jo Ann (an "R" Club member) with her mother-in-law Mary in 1986

Scheduled to appear at St. Lucy's school, a blizzard blanketed the area. Knowing that children would not understand Santa unable to get around in the snow, Pat and Camille dressed in their Mr. & Mrs. Claus outfits, got in the car, and made their way there.

One time an event was set up at their friend Frank's private home where 70 children waited for Santa and Mrs. Claus. Pat and Camille arrived five minutes early. Much to their surprise and delight they saw seven doe and a buck walk along the property! Pat called Frank and instructed him to show the children the eight deer on the yard.

Once Pat and Camille arrived in costume the boys and girls were led in song to "Here Comes Santa Claus" to calm the over-excited children. Next they sang "Rudolph the Red-nosed Reindeer." Once the children had settled a bit, Pat and Camille were taken to their seats which had presents set up all around. The children's parents had given a gift for their respective children, and Pat handed them out.

Shopping as Mr. & Mrs. Claus in Corrado's Market.

Walking hand in hand through town spreading Christmas Cheer.

Pictures with Santa – One little boy really believed he was talking to Santa. They went one-on-one for at least 10 minutes as the boy's older brothers and his parents were enjoying it as much as Santa. The boy asked Santa, "Do you ever get stuck in the chimney?"

"Only if I know you are awake and waiting for me. I get so excited I get stuck and am unable to get you

Pat and Camille

your gifts." The little boy responded in earnest, "I'll sleep all night, Santa."

The expression on the little boy's face was so real that he BELIEVED. "THAT is why I do what I do. These joys are my reasons to continue to be Santa year after year," Pat beams.

The first mention of a spouse for Santa was in the 1849 short story "A Christmas Legend" by James Rees. Over the next several years, the idea of Mrs. Claus found its way into several literary publications, like the Yale Literary Magazine and Harper's Magazine. But it wasn't until Katherine Lee Bates' widely-circulated 1889 poem "Goody Santa Claus on a Sleigh Ride" that Santa's wife was popularized. ("Goody" is short for "Goodwife" or "Mrs.")

It makes sense that Mrs. Claus came on the scene after Santa was well-established. And, just like real Santa and Mrs. Claus, Pat didn't find his Mrs. Claus until his second act.

MRS. CLAUS AND "THE 'R' CLUB"

After 42 year of marriage, Pat had to say goodbye to his wife Claire when she passed away. She was the love of his life, and he was understandably sad and lonely.

Eventually he met Camille, a cousin of one of his late wife's work friends. It took a while for Pat to get the nerve to date again, after all, he'd been married for over four decades! But, eventually, he asked Camille out on a date for dinner. They had dinner at a nice restaurant and enjoyed one another's company. They even realized that they had been baptized in the same church, although Pat first as Camille is a dozen years younger. Although both from Newark, they'd never met before that first date. At the end of the meal, Pat asked Camille if she'd like some coffee and dessert before the check arrived. She refused telling Pat she'd made something special at her place. They went to Camille's home, and she invited him in for the promised coffee and dessert. As Camille made the coffee, Pat noticed special Italian cookies waiting on a plate, the kind he absolutely adored! Pat says that was when he knew that Camille was the woman for him!

A delightful courtship followed, and on April 24, 1999, he married the beautiful Camille in St. Lucy's Church in Newark, NJ.

Since she was a little girl, Camille always told her three aunts, her mother's sisters, "When I get married, the three of you are going to be my bridal party."

By the time Camille was ready to take her vows as wife to Pat, "Aunt number one had passed away, so I asked her only daughter to be in the wedding party."

"Aunt number two had passed away as well. Her only daughter was in my wedding party. And aunt number three was still alive, but her daughter was in my wedding party."

"My mother had three sisters and six brothers. All three of my aunts' daughters were in the wedding party."

In addition to the family who was attending the nuptials of Pat and Camille, Camille also had her forever friends "The R Club".

"Of course, "The 'R' Club" was there, they are a part of Pat's harem!" Camille says with a smile on her lips and a twinkle in her eye.

Camille met the ladies who were to form "The 'R' Club" in Home Economics class in junior high school. In Newark, in Camille's neck of the woods, "The 'Downers' lived on Summer Avenue, Crane Street, and Cutler Street all in the same area. Rose Ann, Jo Ann, Netta, Lucia, and Camille."

"The 'Uppers' all lived on Parker Street. It was Gracie (now deceased), Marlene, Rose Ann (deceased), Ronnie (divorced, living at the Shore and lives too far away), and Patti.

"We always used to say, 'Our ___ is better than yours.' And, since we couldn't get along TOGETHER, we decided we would join forces. And we did. And we became "The 'R' Club" because it was our club. Many people wanted to join us, but we said, 'Sorry, we started with 10 and we're going to end with 10.'"

"From seventh grade on we have maintained a deep, loyal, and strong friendship. We all attended Barringer High School in Newark together. We remained friends. We met every month at someone's house. Throughout school, marriages, children, growth, we've stayed together. There was only one divorce. Only Rose Ann never married. Rose Ann and I used to go out the two of us," Camille recalls.

"We went on trips to see a play in NY, see Johnny Mathis – he was a part of our group, he was an honorary member!"

"The 'R' Club" has been an extension of family; we were all together. At one time, two of the girls were expecting children.

"The 'R' Club" from l to r: Jo Ann, Netta, Patti, Lucia, Marlene, Rose Ann, and Camille, Mar. 28, 2015

Ironically enough, they were brought in for delivery at the same time, at the same hospital, in the same room!"

"We went through a lot of sorrow, but we went through a lot of happiness together."

"Pat met us at club meeting. He was well-accepted. Now "The 'R' Club" meet and go out for lunch and afterwards go to the person's house for dessert."

To this day, Camille assures that they have never had a club meeting without everyone in attendance. More recently they even went on the Miss Lotta on Lake Hopatcong, NJ, near Pat and Camille's home, in June. This vessel holds a special place in Pat and Camille's story.

Camille's creativity and love for "The 'R' Club" led to her making different needlepoint ornaments for Christmas over the years.

"I gave to family, friends, anyone I gave a gift to, I put an ornament with it."

"One year I made them for Make-a-Wish. That year I made about one hundred of them. I would start in October. It's easy once you get the hang of it. It was easy."

"The 'R' Club" got the same ornament from Camille each year.

"Lucia got a wreath and stapled each one of my ornaments onto it. Joanne has a 'Camille' part of her tree."

Camille never used a kit, she created them herself.

"I gave them out and didn't always keep one for myself. For the first time ever, I put what's left of my collection on display for

Christmas 2018. I no longer make them because I don't have the coordination that I had."

"The 'R' Club" whole-heartedly approved of Pat for Camille's husband.

Before the wedding, Camille asked Pat to take her to St. Lucy's Church, "Since we're going to be married at this Parish, will you take me to the church?"

"Which church?" Pat inquired.

"St. Lucy's where I was baptized." Camille explained.

"I have to go there, too. I was baptized at that church, too." Pat informed Camille. It was then the two realized that they had been baptized in the same church a dozen years apart.

"It was meant to be," Pat says assuredly as he looks lovingly at his wife.

Although Claire was never Mrs. Claus to Pat's Santa, when he took Camille as his bride, he told her, "Camille, there is a clause to this marriage."

A 3rd grade schoolteacher, Camille wondered what detail she had overlooked. Pat smiled and told her, "Now you must be Mrs. Claus to my Santa."

Camille stepped into the role that she was born to play.

With snowy white hair, stunning pools of blue eyes, a beautiful, knowing smile, and a melodic voice that makes you take notice and at the same times lulls you, Camille encapsulates the essence of Mrs. Claus perfectly.

The first order of business was to outfit Camille as the First Lady of Christmas.

Pat as Santa Claus with Camille as his Mrs. Claus,
Dec. 19, 2013

Costumes were upwards of $250 and didn't speak to Camille. She knew there was something better, more appealing, and comfortable waiting to be found.

A visit to the Burlington store found her face to face with a plush red robe with fleece that she thought was perfect. The problem? The robe had no price tag. The saleslady searched for another in the store, but there was none. Then, she looked up the robe's price on the computer. Final price tag was $20 so Camille took it.

From there Camille took it to Pat's dear friend, Carol, the seamstress who fixed his rip in the tushy with a perfect patch. Camille tried the robe on for Carol, and she knew she had to add decorative studs to the front to keep the robe closed.

Then, Carol was asked to make an apron as Mrs. Claus is always making delicious Christmas cookies for Santa and the elves.

Finally, dear friend, Mrs. Dunn, was asked to make a hat for Mrs. Claus to finish the ensemble.

Since December 1999, Camille has taken her place as Mrs. Claus beside Pat's Santa. They are inseparable and perfect together.

Pat says, "Santa was always alone until Mrs. Claus joined him. That's when things started to become special having her join him. It is so very special to have Mrs. Claus by Santa's side."

And 20 years later, he still feels the same.

GIFTS FOR SANTA

What do you give the man who gives gifts for a living? Well, if you are an innocent child, whatever you can. And Santa – Pat – loves everything he was ever given.

A bag of buttons

Two pennies

Myriad coloring pages dedicated to Santa & Mrs. Claus

The children's Wish Lists for gifts

Letters for Santa

"I used to take so many pictures with children but never got the pictures from the parents. That's the thing that I miss so much, so dearly."

Camille added, "And we didn't really know the people."

Imagine how many photo albums Pat and Camille are featured. They may not have the photos, but they have myriad memories that add joy to their lives year after year.

300 children at St. Patrick's in Chatham who all came to see Santa and Mrs. Claus.

"I think the gifts that Santa got," Pat said with his voice full of emotion, "was just the joys of the children coming."

CHRISTMAS MEMORIES OF BEING SANTA

When asked what he – Santa – would like for Christmas, Pat replied, "Love, Peace, and Happiness."

A nine-year old told Santa, "All I want is to be happy."

"All I want is to be happy"

"Is that a pillow, Santa?" a child asked Pat pointing to his belly, to which Santa replied, "No, that's for real!"

"You KNOW what I want for Christmas, I sent you my list!"

A boy named Matthew asked the following questions:

"How many children are there in the world?"

Pat hesitated for a moment. He looked to the Heavens and mentally said, "I need help."

And this glorious response tumbled out of Pat's mouth:

"I was counting and counting and thought I was near the end, but then six or seven new babies were born, and I had to stop and start over again. It's always changing!"

The follow-up remark was, "I know Santa is real, but I question Rudolph."

"You don't think Rudolph is real?" Pat challenged.

"No, I don't think so," Matthew responded.

"Well, I guess this Christmas you won't be getting any presents. If you don't believe there is Rudolph to get to you, how can I get to you? I especially need the one with the red nose, because I need his light at times when it is foggy. I rely on Rudolph's light because sometimes it's just too difficult to see without it."

"Oh, Okay, Santa, I guess Rudolph is real!"

Pat explains, "How I get the answers, I don't know. I guess I'm just blessed. It's divine. It comes out. It gets me excited. It energizes you. Boundless energy while I'm working as Santa."

"I cannot promise you a puppy for Christmas, it wouldn't be fair."

"Why, Santa?"

"Because I once tried to bring a puppy to a child, and before I could deliver it, the puppy jumped off the sleigh and ran away."

Another puppy story, has a different ending:

Parents got their son a new puppy because their dog was getting old. The parents took a picture of the little puppy to show their son, Owen. Owen asked, "Is this the puppy Santa is going to bring me for

Christmas?" Well, a cousin of the family heard this story and knew Pat and Camille. She arranged for Santa and Mrs. Claus to deliver the puppy on Christmas.

The parents lived in Nutley, NJ and Pat and Camille live in Mount Arlington. Pat gets up the Saturday morning of the delivery and the day is white with snow. But, Pat, determined to make his delivery, rationalizes that the highways will be cleared.

"Santa has to come through!"

He and Camille got in the car and headed for the boy's home.

The boy had named the puppy Bentley.

Pat quipped to Camille, "This boy has big ideas calling the dog Bentley. Puppy this year for Christmas, and the car next!"

Once they arrived, Pat and Camille secretly met the boy's father who handed Pat the box with the Christmas puppy. Pat and Camille went to the front door and rang the bell. Little Owen looked out the window and said,

"Mommy, Daddy, it's Santa and Mrs. Claus!"

"Well, open the door," they prodded.

"I'm scared!" Owen said.

Pat and Camille were ushered in the home with the box. And, once inside, the puppy started to move inside his box.

"It was a Portuguese Water Dog," Camille recalled.

"Is that Bentley?" Owen asked excitedly.

"I don't know what's in the box, we better look together to see what's in there." Pat responded.

Pat lowered the box to Owen's height, and the puppy stuck its head out of the box.

"Mommy! Daddy! It's Bentley!" Owen squealed with joy.

"I put the box on the floor, took the puppy out of the box, and Owen and Bentley bonded immediately. Bentley followed Owen around the house like he'd lived there his whole life."

"When Owen sat on the floor, Bentley climbed on him, sat in his lap, and kissed Owen on the cheek," Pat recalled.

"When I go back to school," Owen said earnestly, "I'm going to tell that boy there IS a Santa, because he brought me my puppy dog!"

Camille and Pat as Mrs. Claus and Santa with Owen and his new puppy, Bentley

"You can't make up stuff like this," Pat says with a glint in his eye.

REX THE DOG

While Pat was stationed in Germany in the 1950's, "I was going to the PX with a couple of friends of mine, and as I was coming out of the PX, I saw this dog with his ribs showing. He looked undernourished so I decided to get him something to eat. I came outside and gave it to him. That was it, he wouldn't let go of me. So we took him back to our post. I start feeding him and get him back to shape again. He would sleep with me. Rex became our mascot. Nobody could tell Rex anything except me. We became very, very close. He even went on bivouac with us."

After about three months a Sargent tried to tie a rope on Rex.

"Where are you going with the dog?"

"It's my dog."

"Well, if it's your dog then call him."

The sergeant tried but Rex wouldn't budge. Then Pat called him, and the dog went right to him.

A month or so later, Pat was in the PX with Rex. Pat was going about his business and not paying attention to Rex. The man behind the counter said, "Is that your dog?"

Rex had gotten a bottle of Chanel No. 5. Pat's reaction was such genuine surprise that the man knew he wasn't guilty of theft. Pat figured out Rex was trained by the Sargent to take the Chanel No. 5 and walk out.

"So, Rex became my dog. I had Rex for a good 15 mos. In the mess hall, everybody would try to give him food. Rex wouldn't budge." Pat would have to take his own food from his tray and feed Rex. Rex slept under the bed.

Eventually Pat had to go home to the States and taking Rex would have been too difficult with paperwork and logistics. He didn't want to leave him with just anyone.

Pat went to the civilian German police. They had a billy club and a canine. Pat offered Rex and in essence made him a hero.

Like with many parts of his life, Pat's gentle ways, loyalty, and good heart lead him to the best possible circumstances.

One reason Pat and Camille don't have a dog today, "It wouldn't be fair. We're never home!" Fairness is always a motivation for the Ficcios.

REMINISCING

While children attended to decorating the Christmas tree in church, Santa arrived in the choir loft greeted by children. Santa walked down the church aisle, gathered with the children at the altar, and sang Christmas carols.

A warm feeling on Santa's lap turned out to be a child relieving himself from the excitement.

One time Pat forgot his headpiece and beard but refused to disappoint his audience who had come to see him. Always thinking on his feet, Pat relayed,

"I stopped in to get a haircut, but when I fell asleep in the chair the barber took it all off!"

Another time, on the way to a visit, a firetruck pulled up alongside Pat dressed as Santa. Pat waved to the driver. The fireman stopped his truck to see if he had lost his Santa!

A three year old announced confidently, "Mr. Ficcio really knows Santa, he's driving his car!"

Knowing the joy you bring to a child when he gets so excited, he knocks his glasses off his face by waving his hands exuberantly from seeing Mr. & Mrs. Claus.

Pat driving as Santa Claus

"If I see a child approached by their grandparent and the child is hysterically crying thinking they have to meet Santa Claus, I motion to the adult to stop. Let the child see other children come up to Santa Claus. Let them see Santa Claus speaking to them. If the child that is upset sees enough other children coming up to speak to Santa, he or she will eventually want to come up," Pat explains.

At the Ficcio's complex, a friend named Lorraine had a grandchild visiting so they could have an audience with Santa who was visiting the club house.

"Lorraine was so distraught telling Pat, 'I want a picture with her with Santa Claus.'"

Calmly and confidently, Pat said, "We'll get one, don't worry about it."

"How?" Lorraine lamented, "Every time she sees you, she starts crying!"

As Lorraine and the girl's mother were talking to the child, Pat had gotten up, sneaked around behind the child, poked his face into the scene without the child knowing, and a picture was snapped!

A mother wanted to know what her child wanted for Christmas, so Santa asked the young lad. The boy replied, "Santa, you KNOW, I mailed you my list!" Santa said, "I have your toy, but the list blew away when I was on the sleigh, so please remind me." The child did happily.

One of Pat's favorite times was playing Santa at the local bowling alley. Bowling with the children became a beloved annual event.

Getting a smiling picture with Santa Claus sometimes takes some creativity!

At one visit with disabled children, a planned visit had the school leave a parking space open in front of the parking lot. When Pat and Camille drove up, the children knew it was Santa and Mrs. Claus because they had their red car and parked up front!

Another annual event for Pat was the Breakfast with Santa at the school parish center. There would be upwards of 300 boys and girls in attendance all waiting to see Santa. There, Pat had a very special volunteer elf named Peter. When Pat would go to the parish center in June, Peter would ask hopefully if he could be Santa's Elf at the yearly Breakfast with Santa six months away. The promise was given solemnly to Peter that he would be Santa's elf, a position he held annually.

Cousin Lydia's granddaughter said a curse word, twin sister said she said a curse word but denied it. They all pointed to her. She was on the Naughty List for a little while, but not permanently.

A little boy was being nasty during a Toys for Tots event. Pat asked him what the matter was. "Everybody acts up, but today you're doing a little bit more than you should be doing," Pat said to the boy. Pat thought quickly and looked at his phone to see if the child was on the Naughty List.

"You're a lucky boy today because you are still on Santa's Good List. You better be on your best behavior, so you stay there."

The rest of the day the boy sat like an angel with his mother. Wanting to put the boy at ease, Pat sought the boy out and told him, "Young man, Santa really is proud because you are on the Good List." He beamed at Santa, and the mother winked and whispered, "Thank you."

When Mr. & Mrs. Claus arrived unexpectedly at little Jack's grandma's home, Camille's dear friend since they were 15 years old, he immediately showed them his decorative snoring Santa. The snoring Santa had been a gift to little Jack from Camille. Jack asked Santa, "Do you do that, Santa?" Santa asked Mrs. Claus to confirm or deny if he snored, and she replied to Jack, "Sure he does!"

Some children are fearful of Santa, especially sitting on his lap, but Pat is creative and patient in his role. When he learned of a little boy whose sister was anxious to see Santa, but he was petrified of the jolly symbol of Christmas, Pat set to work to fix the situation. He paid a visit to the children's home. The sister answered the door excitedly and welcomed Santa into the family home while little brother hid within earshot. Santa delighted the little girl, but asked if there was a brother at home, too. She assured Santa there was and then continued to converse with Santa. Intermittently, Santa would mention the little brother saying he'd wish the young boy would appear as he had a gift for the little boy. With sister's ease, Santa's demeanor and interest in the child, and the no-pressure situation, the little boy wandered into the room tentatively. He inched his way to Santa's side as Pat resisted interacting with the lad first. By the end of the visit, little brother was nestled comfortably in Santa's lap as was big sister. The mother of the children was incredulous and filled with joy. Pat insists that Santa always lets the children know he loves them, and it's the special way he greets the children that makes them trusting and able to enjoy Santa's visit completely.

Santa loves singing Christmas carols, lighting community Christmas trees, spending time with children, drinking hot cocoa, and eating Christmas cookies!

Sometimes Santa has to elicit the help of family members to help spread Christmas magic and cheer. Pat was asked to be Santa at a school his young cousin attended. She was five. Since they were close family, he knew he could not fool his cousin, but he didn't want her to spoil the magic for her classmates. He spoke to her privately and had the following conversation with her:

"I'm so excited because I got a call from Santa. He asked if I could do him a big favor. I could never say no to him. Santa told me he was very busy this year and would like ME to be his Santa. Santa told me

Pat as Santa Claus with his cousin
who calls him "Great-Grandpa"

he was not able to come down from the North Pole this year so could I please get the list of what the children wanted for Christmas? This allows Santa to continue making toys so every child could get something for Christmas."

Pat's cousin took no time at all saying, "No." She didn't like the idea of her cousin, whom she called Great-Grandpa, taking on this lofty role.

Thinking quickly, Pat told his cousin, "Alright, but Great-Grandpa is disappointed and has to go home and call Santa to tell him I can't do this favor for him."

The child sat thoughtfully and countered with, "What about Great-Grandma?"

Pat responded, "Do you think Santa would want me to be Santa without Mrs. Claus?"

The young girl agreed with Pat and relented. Pat told her, "It has to be a secret between you, Mrs. Claus, Santa, and me so your little friends at school believe." She agreed and promised not to tell.

Pat as Santa with his cousin &
children at the St. Therese School

Then she asked innocently if she could call to tell her mom. Pat told her of course and they took to the phone. She told her mom the exciting news about what happened to Great-Grandpa and how she couldn't tell any of her little friends at school.

On the day of Pat and Camille's visit on Santa's behalf, the little girl winked at Pat and put her fingers to her lips indicating she didn't tell a soul.

She still keeps the secret. In her heart she shares what she believes keeping the spirit of Christmas that will live with her.

SANTA'S SUIT

While trying on a new Santa jacket, Pat saw some children looking at him in the store. He peaked at them and explained, "Santa gave me the wrong size!"

On the way to a visit, Santa's pants split in the rear! A quick stop to a dear friend and master seamstress led to a "quick fix," patch, stitch, and go. Santa made his date with the children!

Pat's Santa visits became more frequent as he got older. He noticed the aches and pains he'd occasionally suffer went away when he was Santa. With each party hosted at a friend's home filled with children and grandchildren, Pat forgets who he is and morphs completely into Santa as he gets involved listening to the children's requests. As a parent observed listening to Santa speak to the children, "Santa really is here." He enjoyed himself as much as the children.

We all know Santa Claus takes the sky on Christmas Eve in his sleigh led by eight tiny reindeer, but did you know in summer you can see him on Miss Lotta, the Lake Hopatcong luxury cruise ship? Miss Lotta is host to Santa and Mrs. Claus during their weeklong celebration of Christmas in July. It's an annual event that has become very popular in the region since 2016 with a food drive,

Christmas tree lighting, cruise, and autograph signing at the Lake Hopatcong Golf Course. And none other than Santa Claus himself participates in these events with his sweet and charming wife, Mrs. Claus. Being from the area, Pat and Camille enjoy their roles immensely at local venues like this. They get top billing and get to surround themselves with children and people who love Christmas as much as they do. And, because it's July and usually so hot, Santa and Mrs. Claus don Hawaiian-style matching shirts to greet their guests.

As summer fades and the frost on the pumpkin turns into December's wintry season, Pat and Camille return to the Windlass Restaurant in their traditional Santa and Mrs. Claus garb to have "Breakfast with Santa and Mrs. Claus." The children – of all ages – love to have their pictures taken with Pat and Camille as Santa and Mrs. Claus. It is always sold out for months in advance.

"From eight in the morning until two in the afternoon, 123 children sat on my lap for Breakfast for Santa. Photos and candy canes were the order of the day for all who visited. Little packages of play toys for the younger children and a more challenging toy for the older children are provided by the Windlass. It's great! The organizers arranged for a little break in between seating's for nourishment."

One special memory from the 2018 event was a little girl who said, "Santa, I made cookies for you!" She came back with one, then said, "Wait a minute, I have one for you, too, Mrs. Claus!"

She ran away again and brought it in her own little hands. She'd baked them at home.

YES, VIRGINIA, THERE IS A SANTA CLAUS

We take pleasure in answering thus prominently the communication below, expressing at the same time our great gratification that its faithful author is numbered among the friends of The Sun:

Dear Editor—

I am 8 years old. Some of my little friends say there is no Santa Claus. Papa says, "If you see it in The Sun, it's so." Please tell me the truth, is there a Santa Claus?

Virginia O'Hanlon
115 West Ninety Fifth Street

Virginia, your little friends are wrong. They have been affected by the skepticism of a skeptical age. They do not believe except they see. They think that nothing can be which is not comprehensible by their little minds. All minds, Virginia, whether they be men's or children's, are little. In this great universe of ours, man is a mere insect, an ant, in his intellect as compared with the boundless world about him, as measured by the intelligence capable of grasping the whole of truth and knowledge.

Yes, Virginia, there is a Santa Claus. He exists as certainly as love and generosity and devotion exist, and you know that they abound and give to your life its highest beauty and joy. Alas! how dreary would be the world if there were no Santa Claus! It would be as dreary as if there were no Virginias. There would be no childlike faith then, no poetry, no romance to make tolerable this existence.

We should have no enjoyment, except in sense and sight. The external light with which childhood fills the world would be extinguished.

Not believe in Santa Claus! You might as well not believe in fairies. You might get your papa to hire men to watch in all the chimneys on Christmas Eve to catch Santa Claus, but even if you did not see Santa Claus coming down, what would that prove? Nobody sees Santa Claus, but that is no sign that there is no Santa Claus. The most real things in the world are those that neither children nor men can see. Did you ever see fairies dancing on the lawn? Of course not, but that's no proof that they are not there. Nobody can conceive or imagine all the wonders there are unseen and unseeable in the world.

You tear apart the baby's rattle and see what makes the noise inside, but there is a veil covering the unseen world which not the strongest man, nor even the united strength of all the strongest men that ever lived could tear apart. Only faith, poetry, love, romance, can push aside that curtain and view and picture the supernal beauty and glory beyond. Is it all real? Ah, Virginia, in all this world there is nothing else real and abiding.

No Santa Claus! Thank God! He lives and lives forever. A thousand years from now, Virginia, nay 10 times 10,000 years from now, he will continue to make glad the heart of childhood.

And for Pat Ficcio's corner of the world, He is Santa.

SANTA'S AND MRS. CLAUS' RECIPES

"When I became Italian is when I met Camille. She's got me speaking Italian!"

Camille's grandparents owned a fish market in Newark, NJ. So, fish was plentiful. On Christmas Eve, the Feast of Seven Fishes was increased and was known as The Feast of the 13 Fishes in Camille's home.

"We'd start with salads: clams, scungilli, pulpo (octopus), baccala, an Italian Christmas Eve favorite (salt cod). Then it was lobster tails in gravy with pasta. Next, we'd have fish dredged in flour and fried in olive oil, we all enjoyed. Broccoli was the vegetable served with the fried fish. What followed was chicken legs, smelts, cod fish, porgies, shrimp, scallops, herring for the Lord, and filet. The fried fish was topped with rice balls, potato balls, and stuffed mushrooms. Baccala – cod fish, soak it in water that has to be changed several times over five days.

Salad – boil it and flake it (no bones), cherry hot peppers, garlic, parsley, black olives, sometimes celery if it's in the house, black pepper, drizzle with olive oil – serve it on a plate

Scungili salad – squid

Octopus salad – served before macaroni

Red cherry peppers in the jar – bread stuffing, pine nuts, garlic, parsley, and a little bit of oil, stuff it in the peppers and bake them.

Finally, at the end of the meal, Italian cookies were served. My favorite cookies were Aunt Rose's."

Italian Cookies

Aunt Rose's Knot Cookies

(The cookies Camille made to serve Pat on their first date!)

Ingredients:

> 3 eggs (room temperature)
>
> ½ cup sugar
>
> 2 tsp. vanilla
>
> 3 cups flour
>
> 3 tsp. baking powder

Icing:

> ¼ cup confectioner's (powdered sugar) sugar
>
> Add a few drops of milk at a time until the mixture becomes spreadable but not loose.

Directions:

1. Preheat oven to 350 degrees F.
2. Mix all ingredients very well.
3. Form dough into a log and spin to make knot cookies.
4. Bake for 10-12 minutes on greased cookie sheets.
5. Once cooled, put icing on cookies.

Struffala

<u>Ingredients:</u>

9 eggs

5 ½ cups flour

<u>Directions:</u>

1. Knead very, very well.
2. Make tube of small amount.
3. Cut tube into small sections.
4. Fry at 425 degrees F.
5. When cooled, use honey and sugar to melt.
6. Spray over cookies and use jimmies (sprinkles) as topping
7. Variation - Bows
8. Bows from Stuffala dough
9. Make bows and fry.
10. Use honey and sugar to pour over.

Biscotta

(Recipe from Carmella)

<u>Ingredients:</u>

½ cup oil

3 eggs

¾ sugar

1 ½ teaspoon vanilla

1 ½ teaspoon baking powder

3 cups flour

<u>Directions:</u>

1. Preheat oven to 350 degrees F.

2. Cream sugar, eggs, oil and vanilla.
3. Add flour and baking powder.
4. Make 5 logs with the dough.
5. Place on greased cookie sheet.
6. Bake for 20 minutes.
7. Slice baked dough diagonally.
8. Return to oven until browned.

Sesame Seed Cookies

Ingredients:

3 cups flour

3 teaspoons baking powder

1 cup sugar

½ pound soft butter or margarine

4 eggs

2 teaspoons vanilla

1 pound sesame seeds (go to an Italian bakery & ask for them by the Italian name, which I cannot spell ~ Camille)

Directions:

1. Preheat oven to 350 degrees F.
2. Mix all ingredients.
3. Make a long strip of the dough.
4. Cut dough into 1-inch strips and form into a ball.
5. Dip 1-inch ball into milk.
6. Take dipped ball and roll in sesame seeds.
7. Bake for 15-20 minutes.

Christmas Cakes:

In addition to a bride, Pat gained all of Camille's close friends. The ladies who are Camille's special friends call themselves "The 'R' Club" because, as Camille explains it, "It's OUR Club!" These special women come up in conversation a lot. They are as much a part of Pat and Camille's story as Santa and Mrs. Claus are.

Marlene's Cake
(Member of "The 'R' Club")

Ingredients:

    1 box yellow cake mix, 15.25 ounces

    1 box pound cake mix, 16 ounces

    2 cups water

    4 ounces vegetable oil

    6 eggs

    Jell-O® pudding mix – vanilla, 5.1 ounces

Directions:

1. Preheat oven to 350 degrees F.
2. Spray 16x4x4 ½" loaf pan with Pam® (or two 8x4 loaf pans).
3. Mix all ingredients together.
4. Beat mixture for five minutes.
5. Pour into sprayed pan and bake in preheated 350 degree oven for 1 hour and 18 minutes according to Marlene's husband, Bernie.
6. Cool for 15 minutes before de-panning.
7. Cut with a serrated knife and serve.

Marlene loves the Christmas holidays and entertaining "The 'R' Club." In 2018, she bought Santa hats for all of the ladies in the club.

Another "R" Club gift is a plaque that sums up the women's incredible friendship that has lasted for over six decades:

"A Good Friend Is Hard to Find, Hard to Lose, and Impossible to Forget"

Banana Nut Bread

Ingredients:

3 ripe bananas

½ cup vegetable oil

1 cup sugar

2 eggs

1 ½ cups all-purpose flour

1 teaspoon baking soda

¼ teaspoon salt

1 teaspoon vanilla extract

½ cup walnuts, chopped

Directions:

1. Preheat oven to 325 degrees F. and lightly grease an 8 ½ x 4 ½ inch baking pan.
2. Place the ripe bananas in a large mixing bowl and mash slightly with a fork. Add the vegetable oil, sugar, and eggs. Using an electric mixer, beat together all ingredients until smooth.
3. Sift all the dry ingredients into the banana mixture and stir until well combined. Fold in the vanilla extract & chopped walnuts.

4. Pour the batter into the baking pan and bake 60 minutes or until a skewer inserted in the center comes out clean.

Date & Nut Cake

Ingredients and Directions:

1 lb. dates (cut up)

2 teaspoons baking soda sprinkled over dates.

Add 2 cups boiling water, let cool (stand 1 hour).

2 cups sugar

¼ lb. butter (less a tablespoon) creamed

Add 2 eggs and beat together.

Add date mixture.

2 ¾ cups flour sifted

2 cups chopped nuts mixed together.

Grease bottom (only) of a Bundt pan.

Bake 1 hour in preheated 350 degree F oven.

Apple Cake

Ingredients:

2 cups chopped or coarsely grated apples (unpeeled) – Camille uses five different apples in this recipe. Use what is available and pleasing to you.

1 cup sugar

½ cup cooking oil

1 egg, beaten

1 teaspoon vanilla extract

1 ½ cup unsifted flour

1 scant teaspoon baking soda

½ teaspoon salt

½ teaspoon nutmeg

Directions:

1. Preheat oven to 350 degrees F.
2. Grease an 8x8x2 pan.
3. Blend sugar and apples, let stand for 30 minutes.
4. Add beaten egg, oil and vanilla to apple and sugar mixture.
5. Add all dry ingredients and stir until well mixed and all ingredients are incorporated.
6. Bake for 35-40 minutes.

Italian Staples

Tarales

(This is a most special recipe from Pat. He made 1000 tarales as favors for his and Camille's wedding, April 24, 1999.)

Ingredients:

4 ½ cups Aunt Jemima® self-rising flour

1 ½ cups water, warmed

6 oz. Crisco vegetable oil

4 oz. dried fennel

1 ½ tsp. black pepper

Directions:

1. Preheat oven to 375 degrees F.
2. Put fennel in a grinder for a couple of quick pulses, do NOT completely grind to dust.
3. Mix dry ingredients in a bowl: flour, fennel then black

pepper.

4. Place water in microwavable measuring cup and microwave to warm only.

5. Add oil to water and stir.

6. Add liquid ingredients to dry ingredients.

7. Mix until paste forms.

8. Take a small piece of dough and create a thin log, "finger-thick."

9. Close the ring and squeeze.

10. Lay on cookie sheet (Pat uses a customized grate for his oven).

11. Bake for 30-35 minutes.

12. Cool completely then eat.

13. Yields approximately 35-40 pieces.

Simple Pasta Dish

(Garlic, oil, and anchovies over pasta with parmesan cheese)

Ingredients:

Olive oil

Garlic cloves

Tin of anchovies

Parmesan cheese

Italian parsley for garnish

1 pound of pasta

Directions:

1. Prepare pasta according to directions.

2. In a saucepan, heat garlic in olive oil until golden being careful not to overcook as the garlic will become bitter.

3. Melt anchovies into the garlic and oil mixture until fully incorporated. Pour over cooked and drained pasta. Toss.
4. Add parmesan cheese and parsley.

"We don't give it a chance to put the garnish on!" "Got to use Italian parsley, the curly parsley is no good."

For Italians like Pat and Camille, this is the pasta course served on a smaller plate. The next course is fish or meat.

"My sister Jean was never a good cook; God rest her soul. One year Claire, Tom, and I went to my mom and dad's where Jean was cooking for Christmas Eve. She's cooking the pasta and the anchovies are cooking."

"Jean, is the pasta ready yet?" Pat's father asked.

"Just a minute, Dad," Jean said.

Then she took out a strand of pasta from the boiling water and threw it against the wall.

When the strand stuck to the wall, Jean called out, "It's ready!"

Carmine smacked his palm to his forehead and shook his head.

Not everybody in Pat's family knew how to cook! But with the recipes in this book, you can!

SANTA AROUND THE GLOBE

Albania	Babadimri
Argentina	Papa Noel
Armenia	Gaghant Baba
Australia	Santa Claus
Bahamas	Santa Claus
Belgium	Pere Noel
Bermuda	Santa Claus
Brazil	Papai Noel
Bulgaria	Dyado Koleda
Chile	Viejo Pascuero
China	Dun Che Lao Ren
Denmark	Julemanden
Egypt	Papa Noel
England	Father Christmas
France	Pere Noel

Finland	Joulupukki
Germany	Weihnachtsmann
Greece	Agios Vassilios
Hawaii	Kanokaloka
Holland	De Kerstmann
Hungary	Mikulas
India	Santa Claus, Baba
Iran	Baba Noel
Iraq	Vader kerfees
Ireland	Santa, Santee or Daidi Na Nollaig
Italy	Babbo Natale
Jamaica	Santa Claus
Japan	Hoteiosho (a god or priest who bears gifts)
Kenya	Father Christmas/Santa Claus
Lithuania	Kaledo Senelis
Morocco	Black Peter
Netherlands	Kerstman
New Zealand	Santa Claus
Norway	Julenissens (Christmas Gnome)
Peru	Papa Noel
Poland	Swiety Mikolaj

SANTA AROUND THE GLOBE

Portugal	Pai Natal
Romania	Mos Craciun
Russia	Ded Moroz (Grandfather Frost)
Scandinavia	Julenisse
Serbia	Deda Mroz
South Africa	Vader Kersfees
Spain	Papa Noel/El Nino Jesus
Sweden	Jultomten (Christmans Brownie)
Trinidad & Tobago	Santa Claus
Turkey	Noel Baba
United Kingdom	Santa Claus, Father Christmas, Kris Kringle

POPULAR CHRISTMAS SONGS
(YEAR RELEASED)

1. "Santa Claus Is Coming to Town" (1934)

2. "Winter Wonderland" (1934)

3. "Carol of the Bells" (1936)

4. "White Christmas" (1941)

5. "Happy Holidays" (from Holiday Inn) (1942)

6. "I'll Be Home for Christmas" (1943)

7. "Have Yourself a Merry Little Christmas" (1944)

8. "Let It Snow! Let It Snow! Let It Snow!" (1945)

9. "The Christmas Song (Chestnuts Roasting on an Open Fire)" (1946)

10. "Here Comes Santa Claus (Right Down Santa Claus Lane)" (1947)

11. "Sleigh Ride" (1948)

12. "Rudolph the Red-Nosed Reindeer" (1949)

13. "Blue Christmas" (1949)

14. "Frosty the Snowman" (1950)

15. "Silver Bells" (1950)

16. "It's Beginning to Look a Lot Like Christmas" (1951)

17. "I Saw Mommy Kissing Santa Claus" (1952)

18. "Santa Baby" (1953)

19. "Home for the Holidays" (1954)

20. "Little Drummer Boy" (1958)

21. "Jingle Bell Rock" (1958)

22. "Rockin' Around the Christmas Tree" (1958)

23. "Do You Hear What I Hear?" (1962)

24. "It's the Most Wonderful Time of the Year" (1963)

25. "Have a Holly Jolly Christmas" (1964)

26. "Feliz Navidad" (1970)

27. "This Christmas" (1970)

28. "Wonderful Christmastime" (1979)

29. "Last Christmas" (1984)

30. "All I Want for Christmas Is You" (1994)

SONGS ABOUT SANTA OR WITH SANTA IN THE TITLE

"Jolly Old Saint Nicholas"

"Santa Claus is Coming to Town"

"Ol' Saint Nicholas"

"When Santa Claus Gets Your Letter"

"Santa's Coming"

"Santa Claus Is Back in Town"

"Here Comes Santa Claus"

"Santa, the Happy Wanderer"

"Up on the House-Top"

"Grandfather Kringle"

"Must Be Santa"

"Boogie Woogie Santa Claus"

"Santa Claus Got Stuck in My Chimney"

"Santa Baby"

"I Saw Mommy Kissing Santa Claus"

SANTA CLAUS IN MOVIES

Of course, Hollywood found Santa Claus to be a lucrative perennial favorite onscreen! Starting as early as 1898 Santa Claus was the main focus of the 66 second modern marvel film entitled *Santa Claus*. Here, Santa Claus is depicted in his suit and beard trying to leave gifts for children who are sleeping. There are even stockings to be filled!

It wasn't long before others started to feature Santa Claus in their movies. The most enduring and endearing film with Santa Claus goes a long way to prove the veracity of the legend of Santa Claus, *Miracle on 34th Street* (1947). A man gets hired on the spot during the Macy's Thanksgiving Day Parade and, because he is so great in the role, is hired for the season to play Santa Claus in the Macy's flagship store. When his actual identity is questioned, a court case ensues, and it is up to a talented lawyer to prove that he is the one true Santa Claus. Not only is Santa Claus real but he lives and breathes in New York City! The proof comes at the end of the movie in a fabulous crescendo that still reverberates today. Remade several times, nothing beats the earnestness of the original. And, it was a movie that the actors knew was special, too. When the 70-year-old actor Edmund Gwenn, who portrayed Santa Claus in the movie, won an Academy Award for his Yuletide role, he replied, "Now I know there's a Santa Claus!" Nearly five decades later, appearing on Johnny Carson's *Tonight Show* in 1991, actress Maureen O'Hara, who was the character Doris Walker, the character responsible for hiring Gwenn's Santa Claus in the movie, recounted a story of her recent visit to New York City for Mass. Five little children followed her out of the Church and tugged on her coat. "You're the lady who knows Santa Claus, aren't you?" they asked.

"Yes, I know Santa Claus, very, very well," O'Hara replied.

For many children – and adults – *Miracle on 34th Street* is indisputable fact that Santa Claus is real!

There is *The Santa Clause* trilogy that speaks to the modern families. The story follows a divorced father who becomes Santa Claus by happenstance. It's a beautifully executed vision of modern-day Santa Claus. In the second installment, Santa Claus even gets his Mrs. Claus!

With each generation, Santa Claus is reimagined and reintroduced allowing him to "continue to make glad the heart of childhood."

CHRISTMAS NEVER ENDS

"Our season never ended on Christmas. Like the day after Christmas. When we went to see the little boy who had cancer?"

"And Camille was reading "The Night Before Christmas" and left out certain words. 'Not a creature was stirring, not even a, um...?'"

"Mouse!" he'd offer enthusiastically.

"These are the things I look forward, I look forward to it as long as the life God gives me."

"Christmas doesn't end."

"I just enjoy life so much, I don't want it to end," Pat said impassionedly.

CONCLUSION

Santa Claus is so emblazoned in the American – and global – consciousness that his presence is inescapable. But that's a great thing! In addition to heralding the Christmas – Holiday – Season, Santa Claus has many roles throughout history.

Of course he's credited with keeping children's behavior in line during the entire year. Threats of Santa Claus placing children on the naughty list is so powerful for tiny tots that they quickly do a major and decisive change to toe the line. No child wants to risk losing Santa's magic on Christmas Eve no matter the date on the calendar.

But Santa Claus has even loftier jobs in society.

Santa Claus is often hope in a time of hopelessness. When a bell-ringing Santa Claus rings a bell to collect money for the Salvation Army, he is lending his jolly image to get citizens to open their wallets and hearts to those less fortunate.

When Santa Claus appears, everyone can tap into their inner child, and children become wondrous at the first sight of the rich red suit, snowy white beard, and twinkling eyes.

There is no poverty when in Santa's midst, no hunger, no want, and no misery. It may be brief, but Santa Claus can soothe, calm, and, in some cases, heal. He's part magician, psychologist, spiritual healer, nurturer, philanthropist, and minister. He's Hope in a red suit; Hope that times aren't so bad or that times will indeed get better. Santa Claus is Hope that there are still good people in this world who care for their fellow humanity.

And even in times of war, Santa Claus appears to cheer the soldiers. He brings a taste of home, or tradition, of childlike innocence and of more Hope. Hope that war will not last forever, that men and women away from families will not always be apart. That on Christmas Eve, they will look to the stars like their family members and look for Santa Claus and the sky and the world won't seem so vast.

Santa Claus is a figure recognized worldwide who is known to be an advocate for children, a bringer of joy, and a harbinger of peace. He is universally loved and accepted in his role as gift-bringer, smile-inducer, and good-behavior warden. Parents rely on him to keep their children in line, and children count on him to make their Christmas wishes come true. But mostly, he has existed and thrived throughout the centuries to keep happiness, excitement, anticipation, and hope alive.

Pat Ficcio and his wife, Camille, do that for their community. They honor the traditions of Santa Claus, raise children to the light, and spread happiness and joy wherever they go whether in their respective costumes as Mr. and Mrs. Claus or not.

Pat never refuses himself to anyone who calls him. One time a nun called and asked Pat to play Santa. Camille said, "Pat, we can't refuse a nun!" Of course, he wasn't going to. He made the arrangements and showed where he was requested.

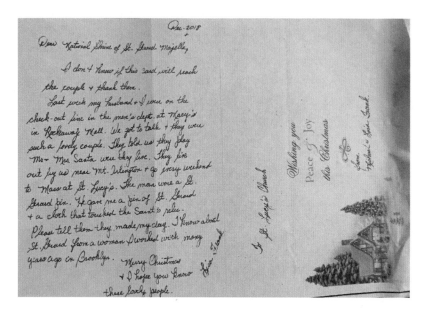

"Travel and distance never matter. No matter where it is, we'll be there."

CONCLUSION

What a beautiful world we live in when men like Pat heed the calling of being the most famous gift-giver on the planet. And, we are thankful for over seven decades of Pat's dedication and service to the tradition.

ABOUT THE AUTHORS

It came a time of my life that I felt everyone should know how blessed I was to live a full life. These treasures I will share with you. As a young child I was in the church choir and things started to fall into place. I became President of the Holy Name Society at St. Rose of Lima Church in Newark, New Jersey. As I grew my faith grew with me. My journey was St. Michael's High School in Newark where I met Claire, my beautiful wife. I was engaged to Claire and was drafted into the United States Army in 1952. Serving a term of two years, I married Claire in 1954. Our son, Thomas, was born in 1956. When Tom turned four years old, we relocated to Chatham, New Jersey.

In 1960 I joined the Knights of Columbus, Chapter 150. I became Vice President of Parish Council at St. Rose of Lima. Later, I became Grand Knight of Parcell's Council 2086 in Chatham. This was all being done while raising a family. My wife, Claire, and I were enjoying our son, Thomas, playing Little League baseball which I was manager of the Blues in Chatham.

I was married to Claire for 42 wonderful, happy years, 30 of which were spent in Chatham. Claire worked for a law firm with a nice woman named Rosalie as her manager. We ate out with Rosalie and her husband Gus several times. After an illness with cancer, Claire passed away. I was heartbroken. Occasionally, I would continue to have dinner with Rosalie and Gus.

Eventually, Rosalie suggested I invite Rosalie's cousin Camille to join us at dinner as my companion. I finally got the nerve up to call her. We enjoyed our friendship and continued dating. After two years, we decided to get married. My son, Tom, was our Best Man. One clause with our marriage was she become Mrs. Santa Claus because I am Santa.

Now, after 20 years married, Camille and I spend time with Tom, his wife Donna, and their daughter Sarah, as we enjoy our life that God has given us.

Writing this book has been a lifelong passion to share.

I hope you enjoy the book of my journey through life as Santa Claus!

Candice Smith is the author of the popular *Christmas Candi: A Guide to Year-round Holiday Bliss* published in 2018. She is an internationally read writer with thousands of articles to her credit. Candice is the creator of Chief 187 Chatter known for her articles about Simple Joys, the Friday Music Blog, and other musings.

Formerly Candice worked in the world of Motorsports where she wrote articles about NASCAR® and IndyCar®. She created and helmed a website and internet radio program entitled *Drafting the Circuits* where she scheduled and interviewed drivers and other personalities in the world of racing including the legendary Mario Andretti, NASCAR® Hall of Famer Bobby Allison, IndyCar® legend Bobby Unser, 10-time ARCA® champion Frank Kimmel, and Indianapolis 500® champion Alexander Rossi among scores of others. In addition, Candice secured media credentials for *Drafting the Circuits* to cover races from the Indianapolis 500® to the United States Grand Prix at the Circuit of the Americas®, and NASCAR® races at Texas Motor Speedway®, Kentucky Speedway®, Las Vegas Motor Speedway®, and Pocono International Raceway.

Candice's articles about her "Simple Joys" resonated with her readership. When she employed the question, "What are your Simple Joys?" in the NASCAR® world the responses became fodder for television and radio spots as well as print articles. Responses from

Dale Earnhardt Jr. and Kyle Busch were constantly repeated throughout several different seasons.

Candice is married to her high school sweetheart, Ryan Smith. They have three children, Matthew, Gregory, and Rosemilee and live in beautiful northern New Jersey. In addition to writing, Candice enjoys reading, swimming in Lake Hopatcong, Christmas planning year round, a passion for jewelry, and spending quality time with her family. A former high school and middle school teacher of history and social studies and current paraprofessional in a K-8 district, Candice also serves on her town's Board of Education that serves a K-12 district. Candice maintains her background in education has made her successful as a writer, interviewer, radio personality, and author.

Made in the USA
Middletown, DE
20 September 2019